RAINBOWS
IN THE WATER

*The Journal of a West Country
Water-Bailiff*

BOB DAVISON

DEVON BOOKS

First published in Great Britain in 1986 by Devon Books

© 1986 Bob Davison

© Illustrations, Tony Whieldon

ISBN 0 86114–775–8

British Library Cataloguing in Publication Data

Davison, Bob
  Rainbows in the water.
1. Fishing–England–Devon
I. Title
799.1'1'0924   SH606

Printed and bound in Great Britain by A. Wheaton & Co. Ltd.

DEVON BOOKS
Official Publishers to Devon County Council

Devon Books is a division of A. Wheaton & Co Ltd, which
represents:

Administration & Production, Editorial & Publicity
A. Wheaton & Co Ltd, Hennock Road, Exeter EX2 8RP

Sales & Distribution
Town & Country Books, 24 Priory Avenue, Kingskerswell,
Newton Abbot TQ12 5AQ

A. Wheaton and Co. Ltd is a division of the Pergamon Group of Companies

To my wife Phyllis,
who always managed to have a hot meal ready
during my irregular hours.

ACKNOWLEDGEMENTS

Colin Harrow, who first edited the diary section of this book.

The South West Water Authority, who gave me the opportunity to work and enjoy this virtual paradise of running water.

Brian Letts, Head Bailiff, who never tired of teaching me the magic of rivers and wildlife.

David French, bailiff of the Dart. A true man of Dartmoor – even though he allowed me to get bogged on the Cherrybrook!

To all my colleagues in the Water-Bailiff Service of Devon and Cornwall.

To dear Carole, who sorted out all our problems in the office.

To the Devon and Cornwall Constabulary for their invaluable help in the dark hours.

To all anglers who enjoy the solitude of the banks.

Cover photo by Joe Ashworth.

Illustrated by Tony Whieldon, an artist based in Devon who has contributed regularly to fishing magazines and has illustrated his own book on the subject of fly-fishing.

CONTENTS

FOREWORD

By Gordon H. Bielby – Head of Environmental Services,
South West Water Authority

To enjoy what you do for a living is a precious thing. Bob Davison most certainly did. He was, until his recent retirement, a much-liked and respected water-bailiff with South West Water. His 'patch' included some of the lovely lakes and streams just west of Exeter on the edge of Dartmoor. It would be fair to say that he didn't just 'look after' these waters – he *cherished* them.

A water bailiff's job can be demanding. To do it well, a man must have patience, humility, tact, courage and much else besides. There is no doubt that Bob did it supremely well and with style. Now, his official duties behind him, he has written a wonderfully entertaining book about it all. *Rainbows in the Water* evokes authentically the atmosphere of the river bank and the lake side, those special worlds where Bob found his fulfillment. There are some splendid anecdotes as well as much shrewd observation on the ways of people and wildlife. It is a book to be enjoyed by anyone who likes a good read.

It has been an honour and a pleasure to contribute this foreword. I hope Bob will write a sequel before long!

1
THE
STREETS OF LONDON

A LREADY the early-morning sun was beginning to warm although it
was barely seven o'clock. It promised to be one of those June days
that one remembers of long-ago childhood: blue skies, summer
clothes, ice-cream, buckets and spades, and visits to the seaside. It was
Sunday morning in a much built-up suburb of South London.

I was on my way to collect the morning papers some quarter of a mile
away along a straight road. Each side were tightly-packed houses, most of
them with drawn curtains and sleeping occupants, with the family cat
waiting patiently on the doorstep to be let in after the night's turn-out.

The blackbirds were singing and, apart from a barking dog, it was
strangely quiet. Skywards all was beautiful, with the fresh green of the
trees against a blue sky: a single white cloud seemed to signify the purity of
this new day.

Below was the scattered evidence of man's defilement. Discarded
fish-and-chip paper, beer-cans, broken glass, old men's spittle and dog
excreta.

Soon people would stir to begin the ritual of cleaning the family car,
invariably festooned with banners across the windscreen proclaiming that
the driver was *Tony* and his companion *Shirl*, or that they had visited many
seaside resorts – not forgetting that the lions had been seen at Longleat!
Pub doors would shortly open to expel the overnight stale hop-and-
tobacco fug into the fresh sunlit air; preparing for the lunchtime invasion.

I collected my papers, which were full of doom and violence. I returned
home, determined to get away from the cut and thrust of city life, and try
and find – before it was too late – a more peaceful kind of life: preferably
deep in the countryside.

My life had been varied and adventurous and I was now in my mid-forties. By the time I was seventeen I had been round the Horn twice and also survived a war at sea. Here I was in South London as Ground Manager for the Inland Revenue Sports Association, living in a small bungalow amidst twelve acres of playing areas, plus a large club that was my domain. The playground of the tax men. Although it was pleasant enough – sometimes – I still yearned for the tranquillity of the country and what I saw as civilized living.

That Sunday morning was to change my whole way of life, and lead me to my present home on a warm hillside overlooking Dartmoor where I have enjoyed to the full a wonderful, satisfying life as a water-bailiff. At the moment I feel I shall live for ever among the kind and generous people of Devon.

It was six months later, in September, when my wife and I decided to visit South Devon for a two-week holiday by the river Teign; our first break for several years.

I had been reluctant to leave the running of the establishment to others; a mistake I realized when a wise friend at Somerset House remarked to me "The graveyard is full of indispensables." I have never forgotten that sound piece of advice.

For the first three days of the holiday it rained solidly, causing the river to overspill its banks, with the surrounding countryside very wet and soggy underfoot. Even so, the complete change of scenery from the city was a delight, and we spent many hours walking the banks of the Teign from Clifford Bridge.

Gradually the weather improved and we explored the area enjoying precious moments in this picturesque county. We also made many friends during our short visit and felt very happy, so much so, we decided this had got to be the place for us to live.

It was towards the last two days of our holiday that we found what we thought was the perfect site. A dilapidated, tin-roof, granite cottage that sat on the very summit of a hill, in the shadow of Blackingstone Rock. The views were superb: Dartmoor in all her majesty spread out beneath the most breathtaking sunset I have ever seen in this country.

Excitedly we returned to London, full of plans for the future, and were determined that the very next morning we would set the wheels in motion for our new life in the West Country.

Our two married daughters received the news of our intended move with mixed feelings, but they soon became reconciled, especially after visiting the cottage.

Surprisingly enough, my very first visit to Devonshire was in the 1930s as a small boy. I was a member of the 12th Royal Eltham Scout troop, and we camped in the lovely grounds of Knightshayes Court in Tiverton, where we spent a fortnight burning porridge and stuffing ourselves with cream. I clearly remember the tiny steam train stopping at Bolham Halt to take us to Tiverton. Alas, no longer.

My wife, who was with the Ministry of Defence, gave, like myself, two years' notice to leave, and we set about getting our new home organized. Builders were visited during the next eighteen months and frequent, tiring trips back and forward to Devon sapped our strength, but not our enthusiasm.

Watching our home being loaded into the removal van was something of a mild trauma; we both looked at each other, not voicing our thoughts. Our bridges were burnt.

We arrived the other side of Moretonhampstead in the April sunlight around lunchtime. Already we could see the outline of the removal van perched grotesquely on the distant hillside as we climbed the narrow winding lane to Blackingstone Rock. I'll always remember the heady sweetness of the moorland air, which seemed to heighten the suppressed excitement I felt as we neared the top gate across the rough scrubland. How strange it seemed as we watched familiar possessions being placed inside the stone cottage. It all seemed a million miles from the hustle and bustle of the busy London suburb. We watched the removal van as it made its way down the lane until it passed out of sight, leaving us with a feeling of intense tiredness and complete loneliness.

That night we were treated to a breathtaking sunset that bathed the hills in an incredible suffusion of gold. The hooting of a distant owl lulled us to sleep after this memorable happy day.

Months of pleasurable hard work attempting to create a garden and road through acres of scrubland gave us tremendous satisfaction. Meeting the local people introduced us to a world completely different from the paving-stones of London. At last we had found peace and contentment, here on this Devonshire hillside, with the help and kindness of these gentlefolk.

My eventual meeting with a man of immense character, and with an intimate knowledge of the rivers and Dartmoor, brought me to my ultimate fulfilment.

Brian Letts was at that time the river bailiff of the Teign, and he invited me to join him on his river patrols along the dramatic Teign Valley to Fingle Bridge. Here the river winds its way through steep wooded hills, reminding me of 'Indian country'. I half expected a band of Sioux Indians to appear on the skyline at any minute. It is an area of incredible beauty and I was completely captivated by it all.

As Brian and I walked he would give me a never-to-be-forgotten lesson on the wildlife, stopping now and again to point out to me a salmon lurking under the heavy roots of a tree. Over the months I became an avid student, and learned quickly: I am indebted to that man who taught me so much of what he knew. Brian is at this moment head-bailiff of North Devon. He stirred in me an intense longing to become part of the county's scene.

I read as many books as I could get hold of, on Dartmoor, rivers, wildlife and local history. I studied every possible spare moment of time. A whole new life had opened up for me: I felt I was the luckiest and happiest man alive.

Twelve months were to pass before I was able to fulfil my dream of working in this idyllic area of Devon. I answered an advertisement that appeared in the local paper for a warden to run a fishery for the South Devon Water Board at the picturesque lakes of Kennick. At this particular period the board was allowing – for the first time – the general public to fish their reservoirs. A private fishing club had been using the reservoirs for several years and now an act of Parliament was passed to open up reservoirs, where possible, to the general public.

This was the opportunity I had been waiting for; but my hopes were dashed when I presented myself for the interview at the Paignton office. There were many would-be wardens, and men of many talents and learning among the waiting candidates. A very apprehensive and subdued man, I sat in the waiting-room while my immediate companion chattered non-stop to me, at the same time drawing heavily on his cigarette. His conversation was meaningless, but I feigned interest for this highly-nervous candidate who turned out to be a reject from the armed forces.

Nobody was more surprised than I to be appointed by the skin of my teeth. There and then, as I drove home, I resolved to devote the rest of my working life to the Authority. I was supremely happy.

2
THE LIFE OF A
WATER-BAILIFF

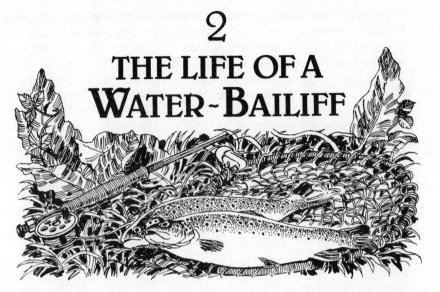

RAINING began almost immediately when the various Water Boards became amalgamated into what we now know as the South West Water Authority. The old Devon River Authority subsequently became embraced into the new set-up and the bailiff service became known as Fisheries and Recreation. This included fisheries officers, hatchery keepers, and about thirty water-bailiffs to police the coast, rivers, reservoirs and ponds throughout Devon and Cornwall. These groups were combined to provide first-class fisheries on the Authority reservoirs. My patch was to be the Dartmoor reservoirs at Kennick, Tottiford and Trenchford: a setting that has been likened to Canada and the Highland lochs of Scotland. To me, no more beautiful setting exists.

I was soon to learn what an important part the water-bailiff plays in the conservation of wildlife, and the enforcement of the Salmon and Freshwater Fisheries Act, not only inland, but on the many miles of coastline that surrounds the peninsula.

A water-bailiff's duties are varied and can often be dangerous, especially when dealing with the determined organized gangs who have poaching for big money off to a fine art. We have our successes and, of course, our failures; like prostitution, poaching will be with us for ever. But the way things are going for the salmon, like the dodo, they will ultimately disappear.

I do wish magistrates would not regard poaching as a romantic, naughty offence. Of course, with the old country poacher, it was sometimes a necessity to fill the larder, but today it has become big business, and the risk of heavy fines is in no way a deterrent. The professional poachers simply put their nets out again and again to pay the Courts, and salute the bailiffs with two fingers!

I should like to see stiff sentences of imprisonment with hard labour – preferably in Siberia! The rape of the salmon has gone on long enough.

Duties of the bailiff

As I mentioned earlier the duties of the water-bailiff are indeed varied. I have made a list of some of the main ones:

1 Sound knowledge of the working of the Salmon and Freshwater Fisheries Act.
2 The powers of a water-bailiff: enforcement of the Act.
3 Pollution.
4 Freshwater biology.
5 Fish rearing and transportation.
6 Boat handling – both at sea and on inland waters.
7 Electro-fishing: surveys, etc.: water qualities.
8 Dealing with the public – a tough one that.
9 Court appearance.
10 TV and other media.
11 Licence checks.
12 Anti-poaching patrols: radio techniques: disease of fish etc.

No doubt I may be taken to task through inadvertently omitting someone's pet subject. If I have done so, I will apologize in advance.

The angler's art

Fishing techniques vary when one fishes still water, such as reservoirs and ponds, from that of river fishing, where not only is there an ever-moving current, but difficult terrain makes casting tricky.

The rivers contain wild, natural fish that are wary. This calls for more expertise and knowledge on the part of the angler. To watch an experienced angler fly-fish is to see a work of art: standing motionless, watching the water, and then with a deft flick of his wrist the angler sends the fly over the head of the trout, allowing it to fall gently. No fuss, unhurried, he plays the fly, tempting the fish to accept it. The fly usually is homemade and is a replica of the current hatch on which the fish is naturally feeding.

As he walks the river bank the angler invariably has to crouch beneath overhanging branches and roll-cast his line, and when coming to his favourite weir, he will change his fly for a lure; a Devon minnow perhaps, which he spins through the turbulent white water to capture his first salmon of the season.

When the 'peal' (sea trout) run, the angler will fish during darkness, and nine times out of ten you will find an Alexandra fly on his line. This greenish fly proves to be a real killer. There is an old Devonian saying, 'When you can no longer see the lines on your hand, put on an Alexandra'.

The tying of fishing flies has become a work of art. There is no doubt that some flies 'catch fishermen rather than fish'. The conventional flies have names such as Black Gnat, Sedge, Olives, Hare's Ear and Gold, Whickam's Fancy, and Ginger Quills, not to mention the weird and complex titles given by the new breed of 'fly-fishermen' to lures with which they fish reservoirs: Black Matuka, Baby-Doll, Black Chenille, Missionary, the list is endless – what about a Dog Knobbler?!

The water authorities throughout the country have introduced a new kind of fishing through their policy of 'put and take'. Although it is termed 'fly-fishing', some of the newcomers to the sport rarely use traditional flies and not all anglers that fish reservoirs can be classed as fly-fishermen. The frenzied actions of some, as they strive to send their lures as far out as possible to the middle of the lake, need to be witnessed to be believed.

Having cast their lures (which normally consist of a mass of vivid colours and shapes, some with beads for eyes), out into the water, they start stripping the line hoping a passing trout will bite. They invariably do – at Kennick – why? The answer is simple. Reservoirs are stocked as often as three times a week from a holding cage, which is moored out in the middle of the lake.

The rainbows, trout that is, do not remain long enough in the lake to become semi-wild and wary. Having been continuously fed with pellets they can hardly tell the difference between a fly and a ten-ton lorry. So they naturally accept the lures being fished off the bottom. Mind you, the trout that manage to evade capture, quickly learn through instinct, and afford the more discerning angler superb sport.

However I can assure you that anglers and small boys alike find lure fishing a lucrative pastime. As a bailiff I was asked, time and time again, by anglers, "How many have you put in?"

No matter what you tell them, it's never enough. One of my colleagues who runs Tamar Lakes, Ken Spalding, a serene, reserved type of fellow, and I might add, a dab hand at the odd verse, has a stock phrase that I know has been copied throughout the region – "Enough for the needy, but not enough for the greedy" – most apt.

On the whole the average angler is a damn nice chap who will stand for hours in the pouring rain, looking thoroughly miserable but always expectant, a bit like gambling I suppose. But he will create hell if he has to wait unduly for his permit. I've even seen them at six a.m. in the falling snow, blue with the cold on April 1st, opening day: shivering on the banks casting their first line of the season. Only the eyes betray the complete dedication of these men. You will note that I refer here to anglers as men, but in fact it is far from being a male preserve. More and more women are becoming 'hooked'.

Just a word about the Salmon and Freshwater Fisheries Act: 'game' fishing is governed by the Act and that is where the bailiff comes in. I will not attempt to go into detail about the various aspects of the Act, this would need a book in itself, but I will just put you in the picture regarding some of the main sections that one would need to know before taking up fly-fishing.

Firstly it is essential to obtain a water authority's licence and the riparian owner's permission to fish. Rivers are invariably governed by fishing associations who, as a body, rent stretches of rivers. They control membership of the association and in some cases issue day tickets for non-members. Other stretches are of course privately owned, but one must have a water authority licence, and these are very reasonable indeed.

Reservoirs here in the South West issue a permit which combines the licence and owner's permission. These permits can be obtained on site.

Specific types of bait and methods are stipulated in the Act. It is an offence to fish with a 'fixed engine'. This term covers diverse methods of taking fish and includes 'any net placed or suspended and left unattended by the owners, any device used to place, suspend or maintain'. For instance, unlike coarse fishing, you must not leave your rod on the bank with the line in the water, baited, if you fish for game fish. It is an offence. Various closed seasons for salmon and migratory trout are governed by local by-laws.

Trout and salmon

The introduction to this country of the North American rainbow trout (*Salmo gairdneri*) has proved to be a commercial success owing to its ability to put on weight rapidly. It can reach a pound plus from the egg stage in twelve months. Most lakes, reservoirs and private fisheries are stocked with rainbows; fish that has become a firm favourite in the daily diet.

Brown trout (*Salmo trutta*) take longer to reach a stockable weight and are mainly reared for release into the county's rivers. The average weight one would expect to find in our moorland rivers would be about half a pound to three-quarters. However, I must tell you that a brown trout of some fourteen pounds was removed from Kennick several years ago. Its preserved remains can be seen at South West Water Authority headquarters. I think it was said to be at least fifteen years old.

A word about the king of fishes, *Salmo salar*: the leaper, so named by the Romans when, unlike today, the rivers in Devon teemed with these noble fish.

Salmon spawn in the late autumn and winter, mainly on the higher reaches of the river, where beds of gravel of suitable size exist in shallow, fast-moving water. Mind you, they will spawn lower down river if the bed is suitable.

The female, or hen salmon, chooses a suitable site, preferably as I've said, with a fast flow of water over the pebbles, and begins to dig a hole in the gravel using her tail to remove the stones.

Satisfied, she lowers her vent into the hole and extrudes her eggs, a mass of orange pearls; at the same time a cock salmon who has been swimming nearby, extrudes his milt over the eggs to fertilize the future generation. The hen salmon then moves upstream and quickly lifts more gravel to float downstream to fill the depression, causing a mound called a 'redd'.

Each egg is about a quarter of an inch in diameter. A salmon weighing about ten pounds will produce roughly between 6000 and 8500 eggs. How about that?

Of course not all the eggs will be laid in one redd and hatching will normally occur after 40–160 days depending on the water temperature. When the fish emerge they are about half an inch long and have a large yolk-sac suspended from the belly. They are now 'alevins' and remain in the gravel until the yolk-sac is absorbed.

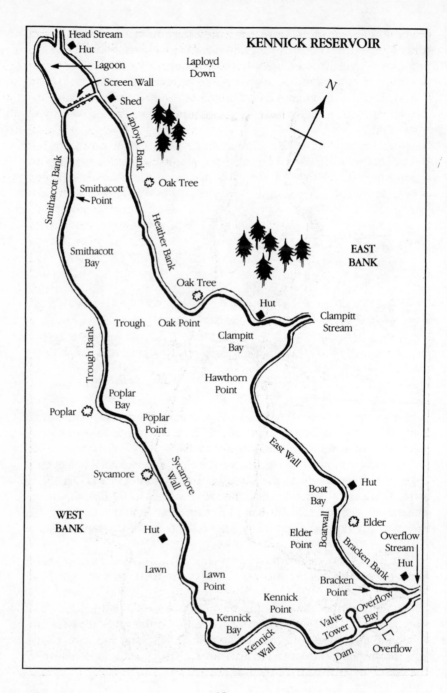

KENNICK RESERVOIR

Head Stream
Hut
Laployd
Down
Lagoon
Screen Wall
N
Shed
Laployd Bank
Smithacott Bank
Oak Tree
Smithacott
Point
Heather Bank
Smithacott
Bay
EAST
BANK
Oak Tree
Hut
Clampitt
Stream
Trough
Oak Point
Clampitt
Bay
Trough Bank
Hawthorn
Point
Poplar
Bay
Poplar
Poplar
Point
Sycamore Wall
East Wall
Sycamore
Boat
Bay
Hut
WEST
BANK
Hut
Elder
Boatwall
Elder
Point
Overflow
Stream
Bracken Bank
Hut
Lawn
Lawn
Point
Bracken
Point
Kennick
Point
Overflow
Bay
Kennick
Bay
Valve
Tower
Kennick Wall
Dam
Overflow

18

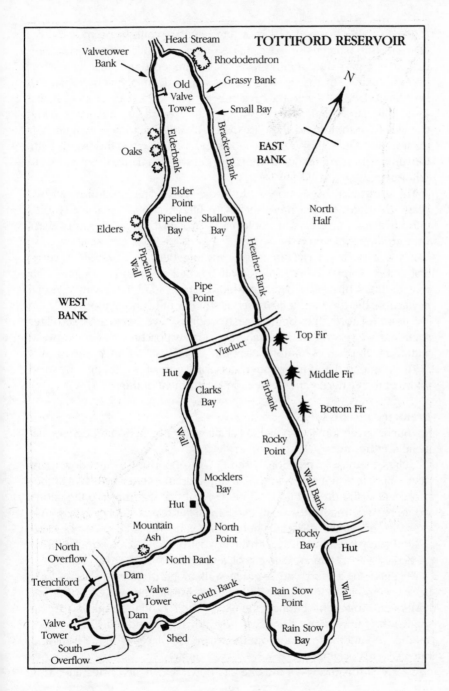

TOTTIFORD RESERVOIR

Head Stream

Valvetower Bank

Rhododendron

Grassy Bank

Old Valve Tower

Small Bay

N

Elderbank

Oaks

Bracken Bank

EAST BANK

Elder Point

Elders

Pipeline Bay

Shallow Bay

North Half

Pipeline Wall

Pipe Point

WEST BANK

Heather Bank

Viaduct

Top Fir

Hut

Middle Fir

Clarks Bay

Firbank

Bottom Fir

Wall

Rocky Point

Mocklers Bay

Wall Bank

Hut

Mountain Ash

North Point

Rocky Bay

Hut

North Overflow

North Bank

Trenchford

Dam

Valve Tower

South Bank

Rain Stow Point

Wall

Dam

Valve Tower

Rain Stow Bay

South Overflow

Shed

The fry begin to feed and grow, and after a while begin to show the characteristic blotches or 'parr' marks along the flanks. When I see these marks on a parr they remind me of sooty fingerprints. Most male 'parr' become sexually mature in their second year and are, of course, capable of becoming daddies. When they reach between four and eight inches, parr lose their marks and become silvery with a black fin. Again the name changes, to 'smolt', and they are ready to migrate to sea. Losing their territorial instincts, they travel in shoals and migrate when the river is high, remaining in estuaries for a short period to acclimatize from fresh- to salt-water.

The growth of the salmon while in the sea is rapid, and in about two years it can grow from mere inches to fifteen pounds. If it feeds for a period of say four years, it could easily weigh forty pounds, and that's without Weetabix for breakfast!

It will return to the river of its birth any time between one and five years, that is after going downriver as a smolt. It is believed that salmon find their way to their birthplace by a sense of smell combined with celestial navigation, but the mechanism used is still not fully understood.

Salmon of forty, fifty or even sixty pounds have been recorded after spending five years at sea. You can now see why poaching is so widespread with the high price of salmon per pound.

These splendid and informative facts form part of our training by good tutors of the Fisheries and Recreation Department of the S.W.W.A.

Breakers and benders

So much for salmon, let's now look at a few law-breakers and benders that a bailiff encounters.

I class them as professional, semi-pros, opportunists and downright petty offenders. I hasten to point out that the water-bailiffs will not prosecute at the drop of a hat. Good Lord, if that was the case the courts would most definitely be overworked. In all fairness, a lot of compassion is exercised by bailiffs, especially here in the South West.

I tell you what, let's take an imaginary patrol along one of the lakes, no particular one, just an average patrol, and see what happens.

We enter the fishery and begin to walk along the bank; it is not long before we notice a lone angler fishing just around the bay. Obviously we have been spotted, for I noticed he places one rod on the bank and, trying to give the impression of nonchalantly moving around, quickly removes another rod and baited line from the water and places it on the bank and returns to his original spot.

We are still some way off as he sits down and lights a cigarette. This fisherman is what I class as the 'Uriah Heep' type. Eventually we come to him, he assumes a subservient attitude. He knows my Christian name which is used once in every sentence.

With a grin on his face he begins,

"Hallo, Bob, haven't seen you for weeks. Are you smoking?" He offers me his packet and I decline gracefully and mutter about trying to give them up. I ask him if he has caught any fish yet.

"Only a small brownie, haven't been here long. You know, Bob, I don't care if I don't catch any fish, the surroundings are so beautiful." The number of times I've heard that remark, sometimes by genuine anglers, but more often than not by flannellers!

He draws heavily on his cigarette, I reach for my little book to record his permit number. I ask for his permit.

This fisherman has been here several times and knows the routine, and yet he now proceeds to search every part of his body for his permit – even the crutch of his pants. After an embarrassing few minutes he fails to find it and begins too look around him willy-nilly, at the same time rubbing his hands over his body.

"Honest, Bob, I've got one, you know me, Bob," he reaches for another cigarette and then with hands outstretched adopts a pleading stance.

I gently suggest he looks in his bag lying on the bank covered by a Barbour jacket, which he had pointedly chosen to ignore.

"No, I never put it in the bag," and he makes a cursory search of his Barbour jacket without removing it from the bag. I tell him not to worry, it can be checked later, and make an appropriate entry in my book. I make to go off and my parting shot is, "Just one brownie then?" He doesn't answer but just nods. I turn back, "Let's have a look then?"

The bag is opened and six rainbows lie side-by-side covered in white sticky mucus; the limit number of takeable fish is five. His face becomes one of hurt and resignation. I confront him about the second rod, which is an unlicensed instrument, and he confesses that he does not have a licence.

This sort of thing rarely happens, but nevertheless it does occur.

Our patrol continues and we spend a pleasant hour visiting other anglers, until that is, we meet our last angler fishing in a tiny bay near the main road, our patrol practically over. This particular angler has not purchased a permit. I had already made a special check as this man was decidedly suspect.

Now this angler strongly believes that 'attack is the best method of defence'. He is a supercilious and loud-mouthed type. I offer a "Good evening" which is totally ignored, and he thrusts an unsmiling face towards me.

"Are you the bailiff?" he demands in an accent that I term, accentuated grammar school, brushing on public school.

"Yes, sir," I respectfully answer.

"Now look here," – it's funny how often this opening gambit is used by self-professed upper-classes – "Now look here, these bushes should be cut," pointing to the hawthorn hedge behind him. "I've already lost several flies – not bloody good enough!" He proceeds to cast his line out into the lake.

I tell him that his complaint is noted; in the meantime I should like to see his permit. He withdraws his line from the water and very deliberately casts out once more in silence.

This I know is going to be a confrontation. I remain silent while he continues stripping his line in: still no reaction from him. The time has now come to exercise my authority. I produce my warrant and caution him, mentioning the fact that he is "obstructing, etc." This produces results.

"I thought the bailiff sold them when he came round?" he murmured.

Now I happened to know that he had fished here before and was well acquainted with procedure. Also I knew his name, a professional man. By the time I had listed his offences and told him to leave the reservoir, I informed him that by law I was permitted to confiscate his tackle, which I wouldn't be doing, only his two fish that he had caught; he was inwardly seething. I escorted him out to his car and when he saw me recording his vehicle's registration number, he couldn't contain himself any longer. Winding down the window, he revved up the engine and retorted, "Harse oles." The emphasis on the 'H'.

That is just a random couple of incidents on the lakes; but the river presents an entirely more sinister aspect. The prizes are greater and the type of poacher is inclined to be more professional. Organized gangs make a lot of money operating the rivers not only in the West Country but in neighbouring Wales and as far afield as Scotland. One particular gang operates from the West Country and has been a thorn in our side for a long time.

Their vehicles are many and changed often. Time and time again they are caught, pay their fines, and are back within hours, reaping their illegal harvest from the fertile rivers. Surely that should tell you something – in this instance crime pays, or seems to. Come on, magistrates, before it is too late!

I have described in the diary section of this book a typical encounter with a gang, so I will not dwell on it here: but what I will mention is one incident of a semi-professional band, who are blinded by greed, and who in order to obtain six salmon of around six pounds, poisoned a length of river, causing enormous damage to future stocks of salmon and trout, killing many thousand fry. After a costly operation in manpower they were caught and duly punished. In a narrative which ends this book I have described at length the incident from the salmon's view.

From time to time bailiffs suffer bodily harm and on occasions their personal property is violated. One colleague was stabbed, one thrown into the icy river, another had a can of red paint poured over the front door of his house. Private cars have been damaged while threats by the hundred are received. But it is vitally necessary for counties to maintain a water-bailiff service: not only to deter poaching but to monitor our rivers, report pollution – a vital service that – and not simply to encourage the younger generation to enjoy the hearty sport of angling but teach how necessary it is to conserve our wildlife.

It is not always the villains who are to blame for illegal fishing. I can recall a responsible, experienced angler who was the epitome of social standing blatantly catching and keeping an 'unclean fish'. An unclean fish is one that has just recently spawned and is protected by law. So you see it's not always the obvious lawbreaker.

The other side of our job is one of enormous pleasure and enjoyment. To walk the river Teign from Millend, Chagford on a spring morning and follow the flow through the wooded gorge as far as Steps Bridge, is very enjoyable and a must for others; or to walk from Dartmoor downstream to New Bridge is to enter another world. Life, you know, is damn good.

Try these walks if you haven't done so; I know you will return again to enjoy the therapeutic qualities of running water and serenity.

Another source of satisfaction to us is to watch young children catching their first fish; the same expression on their face can be seen when they open their Christmas stocking. They then become completely hooked, as it were, on angling. How rewarding to watch youngsters fish rather than hanging about on street corners or becoming involved in the twilight world of drugs.

Water authorities in England encourage children to fish by making concessions on the cost of permits and in some cases allow a number of free lessons at the water's edge. Confer with your local water authority, we in the South West offer you a service second-to-none.

Night anti-poaching patrols are carried out on all rivers and estuaries in the county. The exploits of these patrols could easily fill a book and make interesting reading, or better still a television series. I can recall nights of untold beauty and wonder on Dartmoor and the rivers while the rest of

Devon sleeps: drinking cocoa in the early hours during spawning time; bitterly cold starlit skies and the deathly hush of the Dartmoor night, broken only by the sound of ever-rushing water and the calling of owls. To stand in the vast expanse of the moor looking up at the night sky certainly makes you realize how insignificant man really is.

The heady purity of the air invigorates and even brought from one cynical bailiff a grudging "Life's not bad, is it?"

Coarse fishing

The extensive clay working in the county ultimately leads to vast natural ponds being formed, and very attractive coarse fishing areas they make. Local fishing clubs run these and keep the water stocked with fish such as roach, rudd and perch, sometimes carp and pike. They afford countless hours of intense pleasure to both young and old.

The Chudleigh – Newton Abbot road runs through ball-clay workings and the area is honeycombed with intimate little ponds of great natural beauty and tranquillity. From the road one catches an occasional glimpse of fishermen sitting comfortably by the water's edge, sometimes under the shade of brightly coloured umbrellas, while dragonflies and blue damsel-flies chase each other over the water. The rings of rising fish bear witness to the plentiful stocks.

The bone of contention between fly-fisher and coarse fishermen is age old. Unlike the game fisherman, the coarse angler is permitted to leave more than one rod unattended in the water, and it's argued that they let the fish hook themselves, unlike fly-fishing. Well, each type of fishing calls for separate expertise and skill and I do not propose to pass judgment here: but what I will say is that, in my opinion, the coarse angler is the true conservationist. He returns his catch to the water, unlike the angler who fishes for salmonids.

Many people I have spoken to show surprise when being told of the many functions of a water-bailiff's life. It set me thinking, why not write down a year in the life of a bailiff? What follows is a record, set down in journal form, which describes the events of one year in my life – A Bailiff's Year.

3
A BAILIFF'S YEAR

JANUARY 3

I cleared all my outstanding leave during December and have enjoyed a peaceful Christmas. The snowdrops are already beginning to thrust upwards through the cold earth, reminding me that another year has arrived. I know it will bring both pleasures and problems; but one thing is certain, and that is the enjoyment I will find in walking the river and lake-side banks of this beautiful and fertile county.

Already the geese are pairing and doing their courting on the placid, cold waters of the lakes. So too are the many ducks that are gathered in the shadows of the Dartmoor hills.

Soon the fields will be full of young lambs and the whole countryside will awaken to the new year.

JANUARY 7

It has snowed heavily for two days and I have been confined to the boat-house making minor repairs to the craft. I have observed a number of cormorants on the lake, their dark profiles contrasting starkly against the almost unbroken whiteness of their surroundings.

Ice and packed snow are making the roads very hazardous and it is very difficult to reach the lakes on the moor.

JANUARY 16

A thaw is setting in and already the countryside is looking a little sad and bedraggled. There were heavy mists on the lakes today but I managed to locate the geese and was able to feed them. I gave Daisy, my special goose, a reassuring pat. She is looking well.

There is a full winter flow, a quarter-spate and the water is clear. This afternoon I went out on patrol and came across a suspect vehicle near a productive pool known as the 'poachers' piggy bank'. I made a note of its number.

A cold north wind is coming in and there is a good movement of fish.

JANUARY 20

It has been much milder today although it has been raining almost non-stop. The geese are beginning to pair off now and Daisy, my favourite, has already found a partner. She consumed a whole Hovis but her mate kept his distance. Perhaps he is jealous of our relationship!

I put the patrol boat into the water after her refit and could not help noticing how smart she looks.

The wind is freshening from the South.

JANUARY 25

I am due in court tomorrow and, although I know these occasions are not a game, I cannot help thinking sometimes that is the way in which some magistrates regard poachers. It's largely a question of which one of us is going to win this particular round.

There are still plenty of people who like to think of the poacher as a romantic old rogue who only takes the odd fish in order to supplement his family's otherwise meagre diet. There might indeed be something to be said for the old countryman poacher who, with an eye to the future of his own larder, was often as much interested in the conservation of the animals and fish that he took as were those people whose job it was to protect them. But so often these days the poacher's only motive is greed, not hunger.

JANUARY 26

Rain was pelting down as I reached the courts this morning. I entered the building at 9.30 a.m. and noted which court was handling my particular offender.

Outside the various rooms were an assortment of worried and tired looking souls, squatting on stark wooden benches. The police officers were scrubbed and pink-faced. Legal representatives and clients sat huddled in isolated groups making last-minute preparations. I spotted my man and couldn't help noticing how different he looked, almost angelic.

His usual several days' growth of stubble was gone and he was dressed in a sober suit and clean white shirt. He avoided my eye as I passed him.

After conferring with the Authority's solicitor we took our places in the warm, oak-panelled room, dominated by the raised bench. I noticed that the air contained a variety of pleasant-smelling toiletries and perfumes. After the magistrate had dispensed with a number of licensing applications the court usher called William Jasper Pyke, the man I was there to give evidence against. I took the stand in the witness-box giving my evidence. As Billy Pyke declined the opportunity of asking me any questions, I returned to my seat in the body of the court.

The watery sun outside refused to enter the high windows and as I looked at Billy I again noticed the obvious trouble he had taken with his appearance. Gone was the unkempt look of the gipsy. Instead he appeared quite smart; freshly shaved, his hair plastered down, somewhat theatrically, with shining brilliantine.

He directed his spaniel eyes, and his pleas, towards the one lady magistrate who sat with two male colleagues on the bench.

As the remaining evidence against him was heard he confined himself to long, deep sighs and sad, slow shakings of his head. Occasionally he lifted his eyes heavenwards, partly, it seemed, to invite divine intervention on his behalf and partly to seek forgiveness for those wicked men who had chosen to slander him – myself included. He also gave periodic sidelong glances in the direction of the female magistrate to check that his dumb-show of injured innocence was not going unnoticed. He really was an old ham, and although there was certainly something pathetic about the performance it was not in the way Billy meant it to be.

After the evidence had been given he was asked if he had anything to say. With the ease of long practice he began:

"Your worships, 'tis a sad terrible thing for me to be standing before you on this charge of taking a little ol' fish for me mother."

I exchanged a quick glance with the solicitor who was conducting the case and saw that it was now his turn to raise his eyes to heaven. Billy looked towards us from the corner of his eye and continued:

"My dear old mum is suffering from a horrible disease, your worships, and she says to me, 'Billy my son, I fancy a litle bit of ol' trout for me dinner. When your father was alive he would always bring me one home.' Mother, says I, you shall have your bit o' fresh fish."

Despite my better judgement I was beginning to feel distinctly embarrassed for Billy, who to my mind; and I was sure to even the most naive person in the courtroom, was in danger of making a complete fool of himself with the transparency of his performance. But then to my amazement I noticed the lady magistrate nodding her head in apparent sympathy. God, I thought, she doesn't know he has at least twenty convictions for poaching game and fish. Billy warmed to her.

"Well your worships, I've been unemployed now for a long time" (in fact to my knowledge, he hadn't worked for the past fifteen years), "and it fair broke my heart to see this dear old lady, who's not long for this world, wanting a bit of ol' fish. 'Mother,' I says, 'You shall have your trout,' so, your worships, I found an old piece of netting and I went down to the river to try my luck. I only wanted one; after all, God put all the fish in the river – didn't he?"

I was relieved to observe that the other magistrates were not going to be taken in and I noticed that many people in court had faint smiles on their faces; Billy had something about him that made him a likeable rogue – sometimes. He continued;

"And so, your worships, I catches a fish and I was some pleased. Then these two bailiffs comes out of the bushes and copped me. My poor old mum is dying, what, I ask you, would you do in my place?"

He sat down, taking a coloured handkerchief out of his pocket and dabbing his eyes, his head hung down. He was a ham all right, to the very end.

However he was duly fined and when his previous convictions were made known, I could see the lady magistrate was more than a little surprised.

FEBRUARY 11

A day of bright sunshine and I have been busy preparing for the start of the fishing season on the lakes. I walked the river late this morning and noticed the well-mended kelts* heading downstream for the open sea. I hope they make it.

During my walk I met the squire fishing his stretch. I could not help thinking how contented he looked as he stood there puffing at his pipe in the pale sunlight filtering through the willows.

I completed my duties for the day with a night anti-poaching patrol, but it was purely routine and uneventful. Even so the river always looks sinister at night.

---

* Kelts are salmon, or sea-trout, after spawning.

FEBRUARY 15

Today has been sunny but cold with a light north wind. The river is clear. During a walk along the bank I found the remnant of a net which looked as if it had been removed in a hurry by poachers from the nearby housing estate.

About a mile further downstream I saw the bloated carcase of a sheep lying in the shallows, its eye-less head twisted grotesquely towards the bank. But when I notified the farmer he seemed quite unconcerned.

FEBRUARY 26

I had been looking forward to today – the first of the lectures. Bailiffs had come from the rivers and lakes all over the county to hear them.

As my colleagues took up their positions I quietly studied them amidst the hubbub. It was our first meeting since last season; friendships were renewed. A mixed bunch, two-thirds were in their late twenties and thirties, one or two already were acquiring outdoor complexions. Some, who still bore the bloom of youth, were armed with notebooks and pencils and awaited the lecture with boyish enthusiasm. These were the new generation of bailiff. The remainder were men of years gone by. Their ruddy, weather-beaten faces looked oddly out of place in the room with its pale walls and academic surroundings.

However, there was one who was decidedly a character. I knew him as Jan. Nudging sixty, medium height and as wiry as a whippet, his head was covered with a shock of unruly grey hair that resembled barbed wire. Beneath, a thin face burnt to a blackish tan was etched with lines as if it has been freshly ploughed. From what I'd heard, many a poacher had reason to dread those piercing, hard blue eyes. Jan was a hard man, an old-time Cornish wrestler.

I once asked him what he did with poachers. He told me in his broad Cornish accent, "I tie them up, Indian fashion." In fact he could easily have been mistaken for a member of the Pawnee tribe. And yet I have seen this man strip a fish of its eggs with the same tenderness that a young mother feeds her first born, and my goodness, did he know his fish. His advice was sought by many of the young bailiffs. A very able man at his job.

His 'patch' was in the most rugged of counties where, alongside his lake, he kept pigs, chickens, geese and ferrets. A first-class shot and fisherman, he always sported two or three days' growth of beard, regardless of where he was going, much to the annoyance of his superiors. He seated himself at the far end of the room, legs outstretched rolling a cigarette and viewing the surroundings with a look of utter disdain.

When the lecturer arrived he breezed into the assembly with a sheaf of notes in his hand and a nervous, though eager look on his face. He was fresh from university, armed with a B.Sc.; sudden and quick in manner he reminded me of a well-mended kelt himself. All eyes focused on him whilst he arranged his notes before him. A slight fingering of his college tie, a clearing of his throat – somewhat theatrically – he offered, no, not so much offered as demanded, a "Good morning, gentlemen". He was answered with an assortment of mumbles.

"Gentlemen, today I want to deal with animals that can be found in rivers and lakes...". The lecture had begun.

Dealing with the preliminaries, he was soon warming to his subject. One or two of the bailiffs were lighting an assortment of cigars, cigarettes and pipes accompanied, of course, with the passing of Polo mints which had become ritualistic at these meetings.

Young bailiffs were writing copiously in their notebooks. One old-timer was looking up at the ceiling, picking his nose. Jan was just staring with a far-away look, sucking on his now somewhat discoloured shag cigarette.

After a while names like Lamellibranchia, Annelids, Arthropods, Cestoda, Trematoda, and such flowed from the lecturer's mouth like water over a weir. He did, however, go to great lengths to explain to the gathering, in down-to-earth language. It was not until he mentioned Platyhelminthes that I noticed a glazed look come into Jan's face. He became, not puzzled, but downright aggressive.

"Bloody what?" interrupted Jan. A ripple of amusement ran through the audience.

"Not bloody," retorted the lecturer, "but, Platy – Platyhelminthes."

"What the hell are they? It's all foreign to me," replied the Cornishman.

I observed a tone of annoyance in lecturer's voice. "If you keep quiet I will explain. Ask your questions when I am finished." He then went on to describe free-living flat worms, called Turbellaria, black, brown, white jelly forms. The gut protruded to engulf food.

This was too much for Jan to digest, from that moment he decided to leave the room, muttering "I'm going to the bog – bloody Platyhelmets."

The session eventually came to an end, each of us went our separate homeward ways; and that was the last I thought I'd have to do with Jan until the next bailiffs' meeting.

However, this evening I received a most unusual telephone call. Jan is not the type to use willingly any piece of mechanical equipment, telephones included, so I was particularly surprised to hear his rich accent on the line. The fact that it was more than a little slurred betrayed the fact that he had stopped for a few drinks on his way home. This helped to explain why he'd decided to use an instrument he normally quite happily ignored.

"That you, Bob?" he bellowed. Like most people who seldom use a telephone he seemed to feel he had to compensate for the distance with volume. I told him it was, and without waiting he launched into the story of what had happened when he'd arrived home after the meeting.

It transpired that when he'd eventually got back to his remote homestead and his beloved lake and pigs, his wife had greeted him lovingly with a barrage of questions about his meeting. He had thrown himself down in front of the fire and his wife, noticing he was even less communicative than usual, had gone off to prepare his supper. She was, it seemed, fully aware that any absence from his immediate environment was likely to bring on one of Jan's black moods, so she had already prepared for the possibility by cooking his favourite supper.

"There you are, my dear," she told him. "Just what you always likes. This'll soon warm you up," and confidently she'd placed in front of him a huge plate of big fat sausages and a generous helping of spaghetti in tomato sauce.

His reaction, however, had not been as normal. "Bloody platyhelmets, I don't want they, woman." Jan's voice on the telephone as he described his reaction to me reached such a pitch that I had to move the receiver a good couple of inches from my ear.

"Don't you see, Bob," he shouted, "I can't get away from the bloody things – not even in my own home." And with that he rang off.

Why Jan chose to telephone me tonight – something he had never done before – I am at a loss to explain. I'm not even a particularly close friend of his. I can imagine he picked on me because I'm one of the older bailiffs and he thought that I might understand what he was on about, and I suppose to some extent I do.

MARCH 2

We have had still more rain and all the rivers are in full spate. I collected the new engine for the patrol boat and tried it out on the lake. It was superb. I also stocked the waters with brook trout and they left the net like schoolchildren let out to play, gambolling and porpoising up-stream. I see that the cormorants are active in the lakes and whenever I stock I cannot help but wonder how many free meals these birds have had courtesy of the Water Authority.

MARCH 16

There has been a south-west gale blowing nearly all day, complete with blinding sleet. I was called out just after midnight last night to a fishing boat that was adrift on a rocky bank. I managed to tow it off and secure it at some safe moorings.

During the day I stocked the lake with rainbows and carried out repairs to the holding cage.

MARCH 22

The sun is doing its utmost to shine but it still needs a little extra push. Today I assisted in the construction of a fish transport craft and conferred with the head-bailiff.

MARCH 24

A sunny but frosty day with a definite touch of spring about it. Unfortunately I had to attend a bailiffs' meeting in the city. What a load of waffle! I couldn't get back to the lakes quick enough.

MARCH 25

Today I stocked both lakes with rainbows and brownies ready for the start of the season.

APRIL 1

OPENING DAY! An early fall of soft snow turned to rain and it was very cold although the south-east wind was light. Many anglers had been waiting at the waters since six this morning, ready for the off. They were rewarded with an excellent day's fishing and many trout were taken. There was a good attendance throughout the day which kept me very busy. Tonight I feel really whacked.

APRIL 5

There has been a good run of salmon and peal. The lakes were well attended and everyone was catching fish.

This afternoon I had an encounter with an odd character that is worth recording. All morning, between showers of soft rain, I had walked the lakes, enjoying a word here and there with the many anglers, some of whom I had known for a long time. It was a happy atmosphere, all of the fishermen were intent on enjoying the day's fishing; many had already caught several fish. The car-parks were full, so the overflow of vehicles was parked on the dam that separated the two waters.

I went into my little ticket office to refresh myself with a cup of coffee and to rest my feet. From the only window I had a good view of the lake. It couldn't have been more than a few minutes, when I noticed a battered old Transit van come to a halt on the dam. Out of it came five young men led by a tall, slim, black-bearded fellow with very long hair that reached to his shoulders. My first impression was that he looked very much like Jesus Christ.

They assembled their fishing rods and trooped into the fishery without obtaining their permits. Several anglers who were fishing nearby watched, rather puzzled. Choosing a clear stretch of the bank, the newcomers lined up and started to cast their lines into the water, talking loudly to each other.

Now this behaviour is rather foreign to a first-class fishery – especially my waters.

I walked across the dam towards the gate, anglers nearby watched me expectantly. The waters were very still, a warm, south-westerly breeze hardly caused a ripple on the surface after the morning's gentle rain. It was fairly quiet apart from the swishing of the casting lines, and the pocket of excited jabbering from the newcomers.

Approaching the tall, bearded one I offered a "Good afternoon", and asked to inspect his licence. He peered down at me with a disdainful look in his dark eyes, "Licence!" he exploded. "What licence? These waters belong to our Lord. Licence! – You don't need a licence to fish man!" His words echoed across the water causing some anglers to stop fishing.

After a little gentle persuasion I managed to convince him that while I respected his religious beliefs, the Authority did find it necessary to stock the water from time to time with fish from our hatcheries. All the while this confrontation took place, his companions carried on fishing, watched by an audience of others anglers – all wondering what would be the outcome of this encounter. I suggested to their leader that if he wanted to continue to fish he must obtain the necessary permit from my office. If not he must leave the waters immediately, otherwise face legal proceedings. I returned to my office across the dam about a hundred yards away, with what I hoped would appear to be the dignity of a kindly headmaster.

From inside the office I watched from the window, hoping that the man would show some common-sense. With deliberate exaggeration the party began to pack their fishing gear and make for the exit. The bearded one looked decidely sinister as they boarded the van and headed for the office. There was a screech of brakes and out jumped the leader, who made for the door of the office. I immediately took a defensive position with my back to the wall, expecting the worst. The man looked bigger in the confines of the small hut. Looking daggers at me he thrust his face close to mine – his breath was foul – and said, "I shall pray for you tonight" and with that he disappeared into his vehicle and sped off.

APRIL 8

Today I had a second group of unwelcome visitors.

The comparative calm of the afternoon was shattered by the angry sound of some twenty motor-cycles. Visitors sitting in their deck-chairs enjoying the peaceful surroundings were visibly annoyed and apprehensive. To make matters worse, the riders had all stopped alongside the lake leaving their engines running, creating a haze of blue smoke and acrid fumes. In the past, we have had the odd motor-cyclist passing through, but that's all; the area is used to peace and tranquillity.

One of the motor-cyclists, a tall, wiry looking youth in scruffy leather jacket and trousers, festooned with brass rings, produced a large portable radio, complete with long shiny aerial. It gave forth a cacophony of sheer din and a number of his friends broke into an impromptu rock-and-roll session.

I heard this commotion as I came downstream in my patrol boat and, before I could moor the craft, several of the picnickers were gesticulating and waving their arms at me. It was obvious that they wanted me to do something to restore the peace.

My approach was met by a short, burly youth with a fringe of black greasy hair and a face covered in acne. Chewing exaggeratedly on his gum he said arrogantly, "What's doing, man, something wrong?" His question was delivered in a pseudo-American accent, his chin thrust close to my face.

Firmly but friendly I pointed out that this kind of behaviour was not welcomed here and suggested that they simmer down or leave the area. This was immediately taken as a challenge. "Hey Guys, I guess this squirt needs a swim, let's throw him in!" he shouted and four of his henchmen moved menacingly towards me. To say I wasn't concerned would be a lie; not one of the many spectators came forward to assist me. I suppose one couldn't blame them.

Luckily I was wearing a hand-set radio inside my jacket. I quickly drew it out and called for assistance, at the same time giving the registration of the nearest motor-cycle. Unfortunately for me the battery needed replacing, the spare one was back inside my office. It served me right for not checking before this confrontation. However, the radio was dead, apart from a series of crackles. Nevertheless, it had the desired effect and that obviously did the trick.

The burly one thrust two fingers under my nose giving the 'V' sign and said, " – O.K. man, O.K., O.K. – but watch it, we'll get you later." They left in an explosion of noise and obscenities. But peace soon returned and the geese paddled to the bank to be fed.

APRIL 12

A sunny day with a light, south-west wind. The crowds have been fantastic and the lakes are fishing really well with good hatches of spinners and an excellent movement of fish.

APRIL 14

Today has been sunny but cold, with little wind.

My early-morning patrol was rewarded with scenes of exquisite beauty. The lake was flat calm and the trees cast beautiful reflections that were broken occasionally by little convoys of geese and ducks. By the heron-haunted Lagoon I saw four young deer nervously drinking from the bank, little puffs of vapour coming from their nostrils. All around rabbits and birds were greeting the day with the sheer exuberance of living. It made me very happy.

APRIL 15

The weather is still cold but there has been plenty of sunshine.

Early this morning I checked for night-lines. This is a very old method of poaching where strings of lines with several baited hooks are stretched out across the lake and made fast to the banks. Although the result was negative I enjoyed the patrol. I also stocked both lakes with rainbows and brown trout. I have just realized how poetic it sounds – "the man who stocks the water with rainbows".

APRIL 20

A fresh north-east wind churned the water on the lakes today and the weather has been sunny but cool. Early this morning I fed the fish in the cage and made a boat patrol. The geese are sitting on their eggs. There seem to be a lot of rabbits about this year, and so tame.

Had a meeting with National Park Wardens this afternoon. When I returned I found the lakes were well-attended and the fishing good.

APRIL 28

Sunny and cool with a very strong north-east wind. I spent the morning on river patrol and had an interesting half-hour chat with a biologist whom I met at the bridge.

Also asked for a police check on a vehicle I found parked in a favourite spot for poachers but the result was negative.

APRIL 30

Night anti-poaching patrol on river. Very cold.

It had been a day of mixed weather: sunshine and outbreaks of heavy rain, until this evening. The night sky was clear apart from the odd dark nimbus cloud, as six of us bailiffs, complete with pocket-radios, camouflage clothing and blackened faces, assembled in the tiny boat store that perched high above the estuary. The head bailiff briefed us.

We were told that a particular stretch known as 'Salmon Pool' was going to be tonight's target.

The loading of equipment was soon completed, watches were

synchronized and at spot-on twenty-two-hundred hours, the Land-Rover headed for the river; an air of subdued excitement filled the cab.

'Salmon Pool' lay at the bottom of a lightly wooded slope above which ran a narrow secluded road, leading to a small, private estate, half a mile away. Without a word being spoken, the Land-Rover was unloaded and positions taken up. The vehicle then left for a nearby hidden vantage point, affording an excellent operational HQ. The head bailiff remained in the Land-Rover.

Through the hand-sets the soft voice of the H.B. called each bailiff for a radio check. All was well; the wait was on.

Two of the bailiffs were concealed on the bank opposite the road, two more remained halfway up the slope. Another took the key position alongside the big oak, where it was more than likely the net would be made fast.

Every so often a cloud would glide over the moon, leaving the sky as dark as a bag.

Eleven o'clock struck on the distant town-hall clock, an owl hooted, then all was silent. The cold air was beginning to seep through my clothing. Then I heard one of our group whisper into his radio, "Something heavy coming towards me".

"It's only a bloody badger, over and out," came the reply.

The moon had cleared the clouds, illuminating the whole area when a vehicle could be heard coming along the road. The sound of it grew louder then stopped suddenly. A man got out of the van and dropped packages over the low wall. He then quickly got back in and the vehicle departed. The waiting was agonizing.

After what seemed an enternity, three figures came walking boldly along the road. Reaching the spot where the gear had been dumped they vaulted over the wall. Collecting a net and an inflatable dinghy, they made their way silently down to the river.

Inflating the craft they expertly set the net against the very tree where one of the bailiffs was hidden. In fact one uncouth lout practically urinated over him. A voice cracked over the radio, "Get them!"

The surprise and ease with which we surrounded them caught them completely off guard. One of the men made a run for it over the wall and was legging it to the van. But the head bailiff and a police dog-handler were waiting for him.

I wish all operations went as smoothly as tonight's; many's the time I've spent all night, wringing wet, cold and dispirited, to arrive home empty-handed. But then, you win some, you lose some, and tonight fortunately we won.

MAY 7

Removed several diseased salmon from the river, all of about four to six pounds. This disease U.D.N. – Ulcerative Dermal Necrosis – is playing havoc with our fish stocks. Apparently the last outbreak in this country was in the late eighteen-eighties, and after fifteen years it simply disappeared. This time the disease has been with us for thirteen years. Nobody knows what causes it and of course there are no remedies. It's sad to see these majestic creatures cruising upstream, their bodies covered in angry, red lesions, peppered with white fungus.

However the disease does not affect the spawning or the eggs, and if the infected fish can reach the open sea again – not many do – they have been known to recover completely.

MAY 10

Today I investigated a report of pollution in the river, high up on the moor. The cause was a leaking diesel tank in a farmer's store. Fortunately I caught it in time to prevent serious damage to fish stocks.

MAY 12

I have been watching with interest eight pairs of Canada geese. At any moment they should hatch at least twenty goslings to complement the already hundred-plus that frequent the three lakes. They make a magnificent sight as they cruise along the broad expanse of clear water, with the early sunshine reflecting their shadows on the surface.

During the winter months I have regularly fed them with stale bread and tit-bits that I managed to purloin from my wife's larder, and now I get my reward as they come to me when I call them on the wing.

Last year I lost five goslings – strangled with discarded fishing line: what thoughtless creatures some men are. It's heartbreaking to see the parent birds, utterly confused, not understanding why one of their brood is unable to keep up with the rest, tangled in this killer line.

Daisy is now five years old; she will fly down to me as I walk the lakes and nuzzle my hand for the expected tit-bit. I found her one afternoon, caught up in the Lagoon with nylon around her feet. Luckily I managed to free her and place her amongst four other goslings, who were obviously of the same brood. She survived but grew to maturity with an enlarged joint on the right leg, giving her an even more pronounced waddle than usual. From back view as she walks she reminds me of an elderly matron riding a bicycle. She has become a great favourite.

MAY 16

The river has been in spate for the best part of the week. The muddy swirling waters making their rapid descent to the sea have left behind piles of debris on the primrose-studded banks. As I patrolled the river this morning I found a dead mallard amongst the discarded plastic fertilizer bags, beer-cans and dead branches heaped on the scoured bend. The bird's battered body was entwined with discarded fishing line, bearing witness to the immense sudden force of the river and the carelessness of man.

The river had subsided to a gentle flow and I could see in the clear weir-pool, a dark, green, plump freshly-run salmon. It was jockeying for position at the steep ascent up the fish pass, whose slimy sides glistened in the pale morning sunlight.

The hanging branches of oaks and willows are already showing signs of impending leaf, and from them come the incessant chatterings of the tits, robins and chaffinches.

I picked my way gingerly along the rock-strewn water's edge, to reach a bend in the river where I was to cross. A cover of spruce and Douglas fir reached down to the bank, leaving me with a narrow path fairly free from rocks, although blocking out the sun. I shivered slightly as I met a blanket of damp cold air, but the smell of the pines compensated. Here and there sunlight filtered through small clearings, the dappled water ringed by the small brown trout feeding.

After an hour's walk I stopped and rested on a fallen oak, its sides pitted and decayed. Huge fleshy, foul-smelling grey caps of fungi cluster in family groups around its base. Whole armies of insects were invading every crevice of this once noble tree.

Suddenly I heard the rasping whine of an angler's line. Just a little ahead of me around the bend I saw Ben, a well-known character of the stretch.

A man of sixty-plus years, Ben is short and sturdy with a face the colour of mahogany. His rough, thick hand grasped the rod, two beetle-black eyes intent on the salmon that gently swam in the dark eddies under the bank.

Ben was a wily old scoundrel whose nefarious activities, both in the woods and in the river, gave cause for concern. On more than one occasion we had questioned him on his fishing methods; he was not adverse to the odd snaring, netting and to using line to secure his fish. A man who at times sailed very close to the wind.

Showing myself I bid him "Good morning". His eyes remained on the water; with a grudging "Mornin'" he turned and started to wind his line in, somewhat insolently I thought.

"Have you had any success, Ben?" I asked.

Lifting his head to one side, and with one eye closed, he paused deliberately before condescending to answer.

"No I ain't. If 'e hadn't poked yer long nose in I would have had that there 'springer', you buggers are always about!" With that he spat contemptuously into the river.

After inspecting his licence I thanked him and continued my patrol. I soon approached my favourite stretch of the river; a good half a mile of gentle meanderings, the banks lined with huge oaks and masses of bramble thickets. The home and playground of an otter bitch and cubs. These creatures are scarce now, partly owing to their habitat being destroyed by the constant grumblings of anglers plaguing riparian owners to cut back the herbage to ensure easier casting areas. They thus deprive the otters, who are by nature shy, of their beloved privacy.

However, the charming retired general who owns this beat is a dedicated conservationist, and has been rewarded over the years with an established dog, two bitches and subsequent otter cubs. It will soon be time for the young to leave and I will probably have to wait another year before I can witness their delightful gambols in and around the exposed roots.

The dog otter's territory may vary from sixteen to forty kilometres and within a large range he could have two bitches with cubs. This time, although I waited patiently for signs of them by the holt, it was in vain. Perhaps I shall be luckier next time.

High in the bright sunlit sky I watched as two buzzards circled, their cat-like mewing echoed above. Like a stone, one dropped into a nearby field; I quickly raised my glasses and waited. There, above the hedge, it rose clutching a young rabbit in its talons, to join its mate. I shook off the sadness in this spring morning, when the whole countryside is beginning to stir.

Reaching the sixteenth-century bridge I found myself a comfortable spot and, with my back against the granite stanchion, I closed my eyes and let the sun shine on my face.

MAY 24

It has been a fine warm day, with light airs. Mass hatches of alder and hawthorn flies have provided an excellent movement of fish for the visitors. Even Charlie, the most miserable angler I have ever met, permitted himself a cracked smile, but then only after he had landed a fourteen-pound rainbow!

I have counted the goslings and find I have twenty so far. Daisy has four and she brought them to show me in the cool of the afternoon. She looked very proud of her little convoy as she steamed upstream.

MAY 31

The remainder of the month has been pure routine and patrol, except that is, the last day.

The county saw crowds of holidaymakers all intent on making the most of the hot weather. My duties finished at 8.00 p.m. I was tired and looked forward to a good night's sleep. It had been a busy day.

I was woken by the telephone at half-past midnight. Apparently voices had been heard calling for help from the moor near the lake. My colleague was already on his way and the police and local fire-engine were attending. Somewhat sleepily I got into my car and drove for twenty minutes through the night to arrive two thousand feet high on the moor to meet my fellow bailiff. The air was by now decidedly cool.

Parked on the water's edge was a fire-engine directing its spotlight across the misty waters of the lake. "There seems to be three of them over the other side of the water," said a constable.

I launched the patrol boat and was up in the bows with my spotlight. The water was calm and we quickly approached a little knot of bewildered and obviously frightened anglers.

"Thank Christ you've found us," said a relieved, pale-faced man of about thirty. His two companions, of the same age, were covered in peaty, sticky, smelly mud up to their waists. They were from London's East End.

We got them aboard and made for the boat-house. They sat huddled, shivering and looking very sorry for themselves. The smell was pretty strong. We made a cup of tea and I reported to the police what had happened, promising a more detailed account later. The police and fire-engine left, and back inside the boat-house, over our steaming hot mugs of tea, I asked the man how they had become stranded.

The three men were street traders from Hoxton. They had decided to spend a couple of days fishing for rainbows at the lake. After obtaining their permits they settled down to a day's fishing, armed with several cans of beer and a full bottle of scotch.

By lunchtime they had all caught fish. By that time they had also consumed their refreshments and, as they put it, had a little 'kip'. They continued fishing until the permitted time of one hour after sunset. The moor becomes very dark, especially on a moonless night.

After walking back to the lane, or so they thought, two of them walked into one of the bogs that abound in the area, with terrified shouts to their companion who was straggling behind. He managed to pull them out with the help of their fishing rods. They said they had been terrified.

Still shaking with the thought of the experience, one tried to roll a cigarette, making a complete mess of it. He said they had heard about the dangerous bogs on the moor so they had finally decided to stay put and yell. I asked them if they would be fishing tomorrow. "Yer must be bleedin' jokin'," they replied. I managed to get to bed at 4.30 a.m., dead-tired.

JUNE 3

The weather continues to be hot with variable light winds. Holidaymakers are arriving by the hundred. The goslings are growing fast and I have counted eight altogether. My day was marred by the discovery of a dying deer just inside the larch plantation by the water's edge. It had obviously been shot with a twelve-bore by poachers and must have suffered untold agony.

Words fail me when I try to express the complete and utter contempt that I hold for these twentieth-century savages. I continually fear for the safety of the goslings.

JUNE 5

A sunny and warm day. I have lost one gosling, the victim of a mink. I also removed nylon line that had tangled around the feet of another. How thoughtless some anglers are.

There have been superb hatches of fly, with explosive hatches of sedge at night making the lake an angler's paradise at the moment. The fish are taking nymphs, hawthorn, caddis and black gnat flies.

JUNE 7

Very hot with little breeze.

I met the Bishop, who informed me that he had dropped his glasses into the lake from the causeway. I have made a mental note of the position and will look out for them on tomorrow's patrol. It has not been a good day for angling – too bright and no ripple – so I have advised visitors to fish the evening rise.

JUNE 8

At about 6.30 a.m. this morning I strolled around an intimate bay, tucked into the side of the main lake. A waist-high, cotton-wool mist rose from the water and through it I could see the geese abroad on their morning outing. Heron were already fishing, standing motionless on the water's edge, stabbing delicately at the unwary fish. They looked as if they had their hands behind their backs. Such haughty expressions; but what good fishermen they are!

I heard a sound, a cross between a mew and a high-pitched squeak, coming from behind a huge granite boulder covered in lichen. On closer inspection I saw a brood of young black mink, their sleek coats shining in the morning sun; but they bite hard. In fact they are becoming a serious pest, taking trout for a pastime. I haven't the heart to destroy them, although I know I should. Oh well, live and let live.

Further upstream, a young oak plantation skirts the water's edge and the Lagoon lies beneath the trees. A narrow causeway across the lake separates the Lagoon, an expanse of calm, deep water, shaped like a huge frying-pan, from the main water. It is sheltered on both sides from the harsh north winds that blow down off the moor, by gentle slopes of conifers.

A narrow feeder stream gently pushes bubbled spring-water, keeping the Lagoon replenished throughout the year.

Today the water remains tranquil and still and the reflections are indescribable. Dragonflies and blue damsel-flies abound, spending the day careering erratically over the surface; the banks are covered with a profusion of golden kingcups, visited all day long by hungry bees.

Masses of brightly-coloured buttercups enjoy the sunshine. A lone purple wood hyacinth grows bravely amidst spiky forms of thistles. Among the rocks that protrude from the shallows, a single heron fishes. The raindrop rings show that fish are feeding on the abundant nymphs that hatch throughout the long summer days.

A number of creatures inhabit the oak plantation, including a magnificent white stag. I first saw him two years ago swimming across the lake, his proud head and antlers held high.

I sat a while in the clearing to watch young rabbits, furtively nibbling at a dandelion, stopping abruptly halfway through the meal to scamper off, as though suddenly remembering a forgotten appointment.

Arrogant, neurotic squirrels, quarrelling over some imaginery grievance, fluffed out their tails, jerking them as if emphasizing a point.

Looking down on the water I saw a brilliant, flashing kingfisher, barely missing the water, actually pricking the surface, leaving a trail of bubbled wake. I continued my walk along the other bank heading south, the sun now warm. I wanted to visit another family that had made its home in the shade of a large sycamore tree alongside the water's edge.

The leafy branches overhang the water giving shade to a family of huge golden carp that swim aimlessly in the crystal water; now and then coming to the surface, blowing bubbles that catch the sunlight, turning them into multicoloured jewels.

I also saw the king of the lake this morning as he patrolled this particular area. The Admiral is the name given to a huge brown trout by the fishermen. He has lived here for a very long time; weighing something in the region of twenty pounds or so. I hope he never gets captured.

A swirl just a few feet out from the miniature tadpole-filled, rock pools betrayed the presence of the Admiral on his daily inspection. His long, plump, darkish green body is scarred from previous encounters with the hooks of anglers. Slowly and effortlessly cruising, his head turning from side to side, he sends little eddies to the surface. The carp temporarily disappear, for he is indeed the master. With a flip of the tail the Admiral slowly continues his voyage.

Before returning to the roadside I stopped to look at a fat adder, obviously heavy with young, sunbathing on a rock gathering strength for the July birth.

JUNE 10

Rain has arrived at last and it is very welcome. What a difference a shower makes to the countryside; the smell of wild honeysuckle is out of this world. Both lakes have been well-attended, with a lot of fly on the water.

Today I met an old friend, an ex desert-rat who lost an arm at Tobruk. He wears a harness to hold his rod to his stomach, thus leaving his free hand to fix the fly. He is always cheerful and friendly, and an accomplished angler. How much we can learn from people like him! To think I complain when I have a cold!

JUNE 11

Fine and warm with some cloud and a fresh south-west wind. I made a routine check of the lakes and released several hundred rainbows. An uneventful day, thank goodness, as it followed a late night anti-poaching patrol of the river and estuary which did not end until 3.00 a.m. It was carried out in prolonged heavy rain and thick mist which did not help to make it any more pleasant.

JUNE 15

We have had showers today with a cool south-west wind. During my afternoon boat patrol I beached the craft and walked about a mile to the north end of the lake where a lone angler was fishing. Approaching him I noticed a fine two-pound rainbow on the bank alongside his bag and commenting on his catch he smiled and said he enjoyed the peaceful solitude of the Lagoon. He was fishing about seven yards from his bag and while we exchanged pleasantries a cheeky mink casually removed the rainbow and promptly disappeared into the undergrowth. I was too late to prevent it. My friend smiled, "Oh well, my fault, hasn't it been a pleasant day though?"

How different from the fishmongers who complain when asked, "How was your luck?"

"Only caught three." – the limit being five trout.

JUNE 16

Cloud. Cooler. Fresh S.W.

Took delivery of several hundred rainbow trout and jolly good fish they are too, mainly of the pound-plus class, having taken roughly a year to reach that stage from the egg.

While on patrol at the lakes this afternoon I met Hamish and stopped for a chat – if you could call it that!

Having retired down here after a lifetime fishing Highland lochs and rivers, Hamish is always worth talking to, although his rich brogue sometimes makes him a little difficult to understand. Communication is further hampered by his habit of removing his teeth whenever he is fishing. He says he is unable to relax properly while he is wearing them, and I suppose this makes sense.

JUNE 17

Warm. Fine. S.W.

Boat patrol of lakes, good movement of fish. Valley patrol late afternoon; river looks as if it is full of diamonds, a sparkling ribbon of movement as it snakes its way down the heavily wooded slopes.

Met a lone angler fishing Holly Pool. We sat and talked and took in the sheer magic of this valley in the afternoon's sunshine. The campion-studded banks gave off a soft ruddy glow, contrasting against the lush green of the meadow. Damsel-flies darted erratically over the pool like so many blue pencils, stopping occasionally to inspect some imaginary object for a second or so. All nature's creatures seemed to be enjoying this paradise of a summer's afternoon.

I continued my patrol, thanking God that I could see, smell and hear.

JUNE 22

There are times when you believe that you just can't win and today has been one of them. Robbie and I have been on a coastal observation, but for all the good it did us we might just as well have stayed at home. What I can't understand is what happened to the fish?

We had spent the early morning perched high on a clifftop overlooking the estuary, our telescope set up in the cover of some gorse, and although the sun was climbing it was still chilly enough for camouflage clothing.

Anglers had been complaining of the lack of salmon reaching the once-rich fishing beats upriver, and it was suspected that nets set just outside the mouth of the estuary were taking game fish.

Our sights were set on a series of coloured plastic containers, serving as marker-buoys for nets strung just off the coast, for this particular sea-fisherman was known to have taken salmon in the past. What we did not know was that in the net out there were two ten-pound salmon!

Robbie and I took it in turns to exercise our cramped limbs, allowing one of us to keep constant watch. Suddenly we heard the unmistakable hum of an outboard engine coming around from the headland. I quickly took up my position with a powerful pair of field-glasses, while Robbie was glued to the telescope.

We watched the craft, a small dory, come alongside the first of the buoys and heard the engine shut off. The young fisherman, lean and weather-beaten, began to haul in the net. For the first two or three yards, no fish; then at regular intervals he disentangled bass and whiting, throwing them into different boxes.

The telescope was so powerful we could see that the watch he was wearing was five minutes slow. Nearing the completion of his inspection he discovered the two salmon and he feverishly fumbled to remove the fish from the mesh. He instinctively looked furtively about him before placing the salmon in the bows of the craft, covering them with sacking and oilskins. He then headed back to the quayside to land his catch, and we, feeling quite pleased with ourselves, radioed our colleagues who were waiting at the harbour for him to arrive.

But when the boat tied up they found nothing! The two fish we had seen him take from the net had disappeared. It was only the sure knowledge that bailiffs don't joke about these things that convinced our colleagues that we had actually seen the man take the fish. There was little comfort in the thought that he might have suspected for some reason that he was being watched and had dumped the salmon on his way back to the harbour. We resolved that next time we would keep him under observation every inch of the way.

JUNE 24

We have now completed a week of coastal observations with no success. We have seen our young fisherman friend on several occasions, but no doubt alerted by his previous experience, he has made sure that every fish taken from his nets has been legal.

Even so, as the salmon and sea-trout become scarcer in the rivers we are fairly sure that sea-nets are responsible.

Although we may occasionally have our successful prosecutions for illegal netting of game fish, it still goes on, and will do so, no doubt, until the species becomes extinct. Greed seems to be the ruling factor in today's world. Recently I came across a so-called 'gentleman', a pillar of society, fishing a lonely stretch. He too, had unclean fish in his bag. I can understand a novice being unable to distinguish a 'kelt' (a salmon that has recently spawned – hence unclean) from a 'grilse', but this 'gentleman' insulted my intelligence. 'Never judge an apple by its skin' – how true!

JUNE 26

It seems as though it's going to be a good year for pheasants. I saw three separate broods walking the isolated lanes on my way to the lakes this morning. The hedgerows are densely covered with ferns and ruddy masses of willow-herb weeds.

Travelling slowly along a narrow lane I stopped a few yards from a young rabbit sitting in the middle of the tarmac. It did not move and I wondered whether it had seen me. But as I stood and watched I noticed in the corner of my eye a sudden jerky movement of a russet-brown stoat which had emerged from the hedge. It made no sound. It was uncanny. The brown sausage-like creature seized the rabbit and pulled it towards a grass tunnel in the hedge and disappeared. High on a telegraph pole a large buzzard watched the drama and looked somewhat disappointed I thought.

JUNE 28

Overcast. Warm. Fresh S.W.

Coming to the end of the month now, fishing remains good; the county chock-a-block with holidaymakers. I am appalled at the amount of rubbish I find during my travels. Worst of all are the broken bottles that are responsible for heath fires and broken skins.

Met an American today who enthused about the beauty of the lakes: "You British have just about got it right," he said; but in the next breath went on to say that if this was America they would build a holiday complex by the waters. The very thing people enjoy about the area would, of course, be ruined.

JULY 7

Cloud. Warm. Light S.W.

Routine patrol carried out in idyllic conditions today. The air was saturated with the smell of newly-mown hay; the leaves of the Douglas Fir giving off a pungent, sweet pine aroma. I removed a handful of needles and gently rubbed them together, the scent was truly wonderful.

JULY 9

Heavy rain. Warm. W.

It has been muggy and oppressive today. I welcomed the breeze in the boat as I began my day's inspection. Lots of fly on the water with a superb movement of fish. The Lagoon is a mass of gold; giant kingcups dress the water's edge; damsel and dragonflies chasing each other.

I found a goose in distress and managed to free some nylon line wrapped around its legs; my reward was an indignant squawk. Two cormorants watched me from their perch in a nearby tree, reminding me of a pair of vultures, waiting ever waiting.

At the moment the lake is heavily stocked with fish and the cormorants play havoc with them.

JULY 10

The river has been in spate for the past two days, murky and full of debris from the moor; sudden thunderstorms and heavy rain have caused flooding in the nearby hamlet.

Today, as if by magic, the river returned to its summer flow, and what was more important, the peal, sea-trout, have reached their peak. The river is alive with them.

Heard a good story today from Bert Denham, who was out after peal last night. Bert has been fishing this stretch of the river for the past fifty years and knows every stickle and pool. He is a good fisherman and an extremely kind and modest man whom I have never once heard raise his voice in anger. Bert always wears a train-driver's hat, perched somewhat precariously on his head. This, with his spectacles, which always appear crooked, gives him a look of confused bewilderment. But that belies the man.

He told me how he had been on the river after dark last night, all ready for the run. As he was waiting on the bank he'd heard footsteps and a voice out of the darkness call, "Is that you, Denham?"

Bert recognized the voice as that of the local squire, whose stretch he was fishing. He'd replied with a "Good evening" and the squire had asked if he'd had a touch yet. Bert told him he'd only been out for half an hour and the squire had told him he was off downstream. "Damn black tonight," were the squire's parting words.

It was some three peal and two hours later that Bert heard the squire calling again. This time there was a note of urgency in his voice: "Come and give me a hand will you, dashed peculiar movement."

Bert put his rod aside and hurried down river using his small torch to aid his tortuous way among the many granite boulders strewn along the river's edge.

"Forgot me blasted light, Denham," said the squire. "Here, shine yours over there," he added, pointing to midstream. Bert did as he was told and in the shaft of the pale yellow light he saw what must be the catch of the century. It was a small pink piglet, hooked firmly in the left ear.

49

They managed to land the frightened porker, it was one of the squire's that had fallen into the river about a quarter of a mile upstream. Back at the squire's home, the piglet recovered in front of the kitchen Rayburn, while Bert and the squire had had several tots of whiskey to celebrate their unusual catch.

"My breath smelling the way it did didn't exactly help me explain to my wife what had happened when I got home," Bert told me. "I reckon it's going to be a long time before she believes that story!"

JULY 15

Showers. Cool. Fresh N.W.

Erected barrier in the bay: severe bank erosion. Fishing is good with much fly on the water. Still picking up bagsful of discarded nylon. Luckily the geese are away at the moment.

Routine checks on lakes. The cormorants are active and taking many fish.

Visited the other lakes on the moor for inspection. Pleased to see the ponies are looking fatter. Ideal weather for grass.

JULY 18

An amusing incident today. Certainly one worth recording. As I patrolled the lake this morning inspecting permits, I came across a most impressive character. He was a big man, bluff, extremely polite and exuding the warmth of a huge Teddy bear. He bid me good morning in the most cultured tones.

He was enormous, at least six-foot-six, heavily built and I would say somewhere in his sixties. Dressed in good tweeds he was wearing the finest pair of brown leather boots I have ever seen. He simply reeked of quality. His hat lay on the bank with his fishing bag, and the light breeze teased his thin grey hair into wispy strands as he reeled in his line.

I suggested he put on a March Brown this morning and towards lunch time try a Pheasant-tail-nymph. He thanked me, and as I inspected his licence I was not surprised to learn that he was a peer of the realm.

After spending a respectable amount of time with him, putting him wise to the movement of fish in this particular water, I continued my patrol.

The morning passed uneventfully; I met the usual few dedicated anglers who could always be found fishing this lake, some had caught fish, some had not. Nevertheless they all seemed to be content in the warm sunshine, backed with huge fleecy clouds, affording enough shadow on the water for their lines. I then decided to do a boat patrol of the larger lake before lunch. I returned to my office after completing the patrol when a rather old Morris Minor drew up. Out 'fumbled' a frail, elderly little man who was obviously far from happy about something. He asked me hesitantly if I was the bailiff, which confirmed what was already fairly obvious, that he was no fisherman. When I told him I was he looked very relieved.

He explained with a great amount of foot-shuffling and head-shaking that he and his wife, who were both keen bird-watchers, had parked at the far end of the lake. Through their binoculars they had been studying one of the cormorants that often visit the water – much, I might add, to the annoyance of the anglers. Until this moment I was under the impression that my elderly visitor was alone in the car but now I noticed he had a passenger, a lady, equally old and frail. The reason she had escaped my notice was that every time I glanced in her direction she made a determined effort to hide herself underneath the car seat.

The little man, getting more and more uncomfortable as he struggled on with his story, exhibited an obvious reluctance to go into details. He told me that his wife had seen something "not very nice – not the sort of thing you'd expect at a fishery," he added, as if that was sufficient explanation.

When I pressed him on exactly what it was she had seen, all he would say was that he thought it would be a good idea if I visited the other end of the lake, where, he said, some "person", and the way he used the word left me in no doubt that it was hardly meant to be a compliment, was "acting rather peculiarly".

Nothing surprizes me after all these years, but before I could gain any further details, he made for the door, still mumbling to himself. As he got back into his car I managed to catch what I thought to be the word "naked", and also a shrill cry of "disgusting" from the tiny figure in the passenger seat.

I climbed into my car, drove the two miles to the other end of the lake, and then walked back along the bank roughly to the spot indicated by the old man. Turning a sharp bend I suddenly came across the sight that had so disturbed the old couple.

Completely naked, except for his hat on his head set at a rakish angle, was his Lordship – completely unabashed. Spread out on the heather-covered bank were his clothes and I was amazed to see a pair of brightly coloured Y-fronts fluttering from a nearby hawthorn bush.

"Hello," he said grinning, "I have caught a beauty – look under my bag." He cast his line once again out into the water, not attempting to explain his odd behaviour. Sure enough the rainbow trout was a fine specimen, I should say it weighed about eleven pounds, in fact, later it was found to be eleven pounds ten ounces.

I complimented him on the fish, but then I felt I had to insist that he put his trousers on. I noticed his ample form was covered in a mat of ginger-grey hairs, and that ridiculous hat perched on his head gave him a look of incongruous eccentricity. His little member was shrivelled and purple in the freshening breeze.

"I don't know if they're dry yet, old chap?" he said picking up the wet trousers. Still wearing his hat decorated with brightly covered flies, he disappeared into his underpants. I thought, he only wants a banjo now!. The trousers, although still wet, were also put on and, taking a swig from a silver flask retrieved from a back pocket, he told me his story.

"I put on a March Brown and fished for about half an hour; I then decided to have a pipe, but like a damn fool I put the rod under my arm, and at that precise moment there was a terrific jerk. I knew I was into something big, but in my panic I slipped and went into the water (it's about fifteen feet deep at that point!) but the blighter was still on – at least it's a good size fish. Listen, be a good chap, ring my hotel and get them to send some fresh togs up to me will you? I say, these are dashed uncomfortable you know," he said, pulling a leg of the clinging trousers with his thumb and forefinger.

When his fresh gear eventually arrived he went on his way, happy with his catch.

Fishing, like a Turkish bath, is indeed a good leveller!

JULY 27

Overcast. Showers. S.W.

We had a field exercise today. In four teams each of three men we reported to HQ and collected Land-Rovers and fish-tanks. A routine check of vehicles and equipment preceded collection of oxygen. Having been briefed we began our journey to the hatchery at the other end of the county.

Each team had been handed two sealed envelopes containing orders. These read: *First, all proceed to hatchery and collect a number of brown trout, making sure all the necessary precautions are taken for the safe transportation of fish, etc.*

Having secured our loads we then opened another envelope which gave a map-reference: we worked out our positions and proceeded.

Now if you've plotted your area correctly (which in this instance was the upper reaches of a river on the high moor) you are then instructed to release a number of brown trout into the river. One team found themselves at the foot of a well-known tor and it was painfully obvious to them that they were not expected to stock *that* with fish. Thus they had to revise their calculations and, of course, lose marks and time. We had then to complete a number of other tasks covering law enforcement, pollution, and stocking of rivers and lakes. We finished the day dead-tired but it had been an experience.

AUGUST 3

A month of showers and strong winds, temperatures about normal.

Several fishing competitions held with some very good 'bags' taken. The county is pretty crowded with visitors, all seemed to be enjoying themselves. Met French, German and Dutch visitors. I must record a rather amusing encounter that occurred today involving one of them.

During the morning, more and more holidaymakers and visitors had been arriving at the lakes. By two o'clock the area was packed. The sun had decided to shine after a miserable start, and the many hundreds of people had left their cars and were settled in a variety of chairs and air-filled cushions, all lying back soaking up the welcome sun. There was little noise, no radios blaring, and even the children seemed to be content just to lazily play, all enjoying the superb moorland air. The lakes were sparkling and complete with attendant families of Canada geese who cheerfully accepted offerings from the children.

I was walking across the dam, stopping to exchange a word here and there, when a small coach drew up alongside me requesting a parking place. He was directed to a reserved place. After a short while a party of about thirty people trooped on to the dam. They were all Dutch, armed with cameras, field-glasses, handbags and knickerbockers, all intent to out-talk each other. Needless to say, they created a point of interest to the resident visitors.

One female, undoubtedly the leader, acted as spokesperson for the party. She looked extremely formidable. In her early fifties, squat with beautiful blonde hair tied severely in coiled plaits at the back of her head, she had a matronly face devoid of make-up. She was dressed in rather a masculine two-piece suit of light tweed and her sturdy legs, the shape of two quart beer-bottles upside down, were firmly set in a pair of 'no-nonsense', flat-heeled shoes. Strung around her neck were a pair of magnificent Zeiss field-glasses. In fact, as I watched her, with feet astride looking upstream, I thought she would be more at home on the bridge of a destroyer in mid-Atlantic!

Every so often one of the party would ask her a question, at which she waved an answer in a loud, guttural voice. The other holidaymakers were warming to this added bonus of entertainment, especially when the matron discovered that I was the bailiff-warden and made a bee-line for me.

"Gut afternoon, please, you tell me about this fishing here?" she asked with a beaming smile; I noticed she sported a large brown mole on her chin. Her friends gathered round and I tried to explain the rudiments of fly-fishing. In Holland, and also in Germany, there are no restrictions on baits and anglers when fishing for game fish, use bread and cheese, maggots, worms, spinners – anything goes.

Here in Britain, I told the visitors, we use artificial flies because it requires more skill to catch fish, and it's more sporting for the trout, at least, so we believe. But the large Dutch lady could not seem to understand. I removed a couple of flies from my hat and invited her to examine them. Great interest was shown, and she duly translated to her friends the merits of a Bloody Butcher, Zulu and a Greenwell's Glory. She was now obviously enjoying the possession of her new-found knowledge and seemed reluctant to move away from the subject, questioning me about materials, colours and patterns, and then passing on the information to the rest of her party who by this time could be seen, even by the most insensitive observer, to be rapidly becoming bored.

However they were either too polite or afraid, possibly remembering her bulk and demeanour, to make any attempt to move on. Suddenly their leader broke off from her questioning and took several purposeful strides away from the main party. Grasping her glasses she began to peer intently at an angler who had arrived as we had been talking and had now begun fishing off the bank about thirty yards away.

Her concentration on the man was intense as she screwed up her eyes and face in what seemed a determined effort to take advantage of every last particle of magnification that the binoculars could give her. We were all fascinated at the interest she seemed to be taking in the man's action as he stood there, first back, and then forward-casting over the water.

Finally she had had enough. She lowered the binoculars, and as she did so I noticed, to my surprise, that she appeared to be profoundly crestfallen. I did not feel in a position to ask her for an explanation of her obvious disappointment at what she had seen, but then I did not have to. "Ach," she began, in a voice which carried around the lake-shore. "Ach so. I have looked, so very hard I have looked, and still I cannot see his flies!"

The remark brought hoots of laughter from the residents who had been watching and listening to the lady's performance. But after a brief look at her little knot of friends that betrayed only a moment's confusion, she obviously decided that this was an example of the strange British sense of humour and began to join in the general laughter.

AUGUST 5

Arrived home today to be told by my wife that, "the man with the funny voice has been on the phone." I knew right away who she meant. Hamish had called to tell me that he had mislaid his teeth while out fishing on the lakes today and asked if I would keep a look out for them. I gather from his message that the last-known resting-place of Hamish's choppers is the third hazel bush past Bishop's Ripple.

AUGUST 6

Began my early morning patrol of lakes at six-thirty, searching for night-lines. A light, wispy mist hung eerily over the water and I listened to the dull plops of fish taking unwary flies. The Canada geese were awake, sailing across the lake like some forgotten armada. The herons were already fishing, absent-minded judges, stabbing the waters as though making a point of order.

But my mind was quickly drawn out of my reverie as I approached Bishop's Ripple and remembered Hamish's teeth. All I found was a half-empty bottle of Highland Cream. It is not surprising that Hamish's teeth have gone missing.

AUGUST 8

Received a visit today from two men who told me they were the Authority's auditors. After what happened to one of them I doubt I shall see them again for some time.

The weather couldn't seem to make up its mind whether to stay sunny and dry, or pelt down with rain. First the sun shone brilliantly from a blue sky, warm and comforting, and then within minutes, dark nimbus clouds would blunder forward and completely blot out the sun.

At 11.00 a.m. I had just finished my patrol of the lake and returned to my little office when a car arrived containing two men. From the look of them it was obvious to me that they didn't intend to fish. Both were dressed in formal suits, complete with umbrellas, hats and stern, unsmiling faces. They both carried leather briefcases.

They explained in a rather condescending manner that they were the Water Authority's auditors and that they had come to check the anglers' licences. I confessed that this procedure was something new to me and, while they began to write their lists and to check receipts, I volunteered that I had, in fact, just completed my licence check and could perhaps save them the trouble of walking the same two miles or so around the lake. This was met with, first, a glance at each other and then finally, with a frosty look in my direction, a terse "No thank you".

To say I was a little put-out by their attitude would have been putting it mildly; however I pointed out that as the anglers were pretty scattered, perhaps they might like to be transported in my little dory craft. Only then did I see a glimmer of gratitude.

The sun was by now at its highest, and as we climbed aboard the flies began their torture.

Bill and Ben, whom I had already nicknamed in my mind, sat side-by-side midships as we headed upstream. It began to rain gently. What a picture it made: Bill and Ben sitting bolt upright, silent, with umbrellas held high. I could see their eyes darting from side-to-side, taking in the scene as we chugged along. I couldn't help imagining that here I was, taking two missionaries up the Zambezi.

Our first angler was fishing the Bay where a notorious deep, rocky ledge ran out from the point. I warned my passengers not to make a move out of the boat until I secured, for a sudden movement in this frail craft would send it spinning away from the bank.

Easing off the throttle we began to glide gently towards the bank, but Bill was already on his feet. Complete with hat, glasses, briefcase and, believe it or not, his umbrella held high, he attempted to walk off the boat. As his feet touched the bank, the craft swung wildly off the shore. Bill dropped like a stone into the lake, surfacing a few seconds later with water pouring from every orifice. His spectacles were now twisted at a grotesque angle while the umbrella floated downstream like an inverted mushroom.

Bill quickly scrambled ashore and, with typical British aplomb, announced his identity to the astonished angler and asked to check his licence. I'd no idea what the fisherman must have thought of this strange visitation, but I had to admit that my heart warmed to Bill as he checked the licence against his dripping notes.

AUGUST 12

It looks as though Robbie has cracked it. The mystery of the missing salmon that we saw being taken during our coastal observation, but which never reached the harbour, looks as if it has been solved. It was achieved not through spending hours on a cramped clifftop with eyes glued to a telescope, but as the result of a leisurely swim in the estuary. But I mustn't be too optimistic, we still have to catch the man with the booty.

The weather was glorious today and both Robbie and I decided to take a swim in the estuary as a relaxation from observations we had been making. It was slack-water and the narrow, sandy beach began to fill with holidaymakers. Robbie is an accomplished swimmer and soon reached the far side of the buoy-marked channel. I ventured only as far as midstream and enjoyed the complete relaxation of floating, looking upwards to the wide expanse of vivid blue sky. I did notice however that Robbie had stopped, and was resting, holding on to the rusty cage of the buoy and removing what to me looked like a mass of brown paper. After a while he swam towards me urging me to come ashore. I could tell that he was excited as he headed for the beach with his immaculate crawl.

We arrived somewhat breathless amid the noisy crowd of bathers, picking our way gingerly over the mass of sprawling bodies to reach our vehicle parked nearby in a friend's yard. The heat of the flagstones burned our damp, sand-encrusted feet as we thankfully hopped into the car. Only after lighting a cigarette did Robbie start to talk about his find. What he had discovered was two salmon in a small sack, stowed inside the buoy. "And we know, don't we, who's been hiding them in there?" he said. It was the answer to our riddle.

As the tide was due to turn in twenty minutes we lost no time in reporting back to headquarters. It wasn't possible, in the short time, to muster a full team but Robbie and I returned to the landing stage, only to be seen and recognized by the offending fisherman, who was about to put to sea. He insolently gave us a wave of recognition with his jerseyed arm, which ended in a two-fingered salute. We concede defeat today but only temporarily.

AUGUST 16

We got the bugger. No doubt about it this time. The head-bailiff had found a superb vantage point that commanded a wide view, not only of the suspect net, but also of the channel and landing jetty. We took up our positions in the early hours this morning.

The two-fingered gesture still rankled as we waited for our suspect to inspect his nets. The head-bailiff, who had already been out to the net had the extraordinary luck of finding a ten-pound salmon trapped in the mesh. He had cut off part of its dorsal fin and put it into his notebook. He then put the salmon back into the gill net.

There were a couple of early risers out swimming in a moderate swell while seawards, a gaggle of gulls were fighting noisily over the contents of a tanker's slop-buckets. I was studying a family of shags drying their wings after a recent feast when the crackle of the radio quickly reminded me why I was there. The suspect's boat had been spotted.

Reaching the pattern of nets the fisherman quickly and expertly removed the captured fish, throwing them into a scruffy wooden box. We watched him remove the salmon with seeming indifference; however, this was placed into a small brown sandbag. He completed his examination in a short time and put out to sea before turning the boat in a lazy circle heading for the shore. An escort of expectant gulls hovered over the stern.

With agonizing slowness he entered the swept channel and steamed towards the landing stage, not even glancing at the marker-buoy where we had a craft ready to pounce.

But we had other men at the quay to welcome him. A quick message on the radio alerted them that the prize was on board this time. Hurriedly joining our colleagues on the shore, we arrived just as he was being questioned, vehemently denying all knowledge of the salmon. "I found the bloody thing hanging from a buoy – now prove it you bastards."

It gave me intense satisfaction when the head-bailiff confronted him with the missing piece of dorsal fin. The fisherman's retort was "Oh well you bastards, it's only one. I can afford to give it to you this time, but you're not so bloody clever, I'll beat you in the end."

As I left I couldn't help but return his previous salutation with two sunburnt fingers.

SEPTEMBER 1

What magic is the month of September: the soft sunshine adds a mellow look to ravaged countryside that has borne the brunt of thousands of visitors who have roamed and played over its gentle contours. Now, with most of the holidaymakers departed, a kind of sigh seems to come forth from the weary county whose air is at last losing the choking, acrid fumes from the invasion of the motor car.

I walked the rivers and lakes this month in comparative peace; and for company I have all of nature's creatures. But my happiness was on this day to be shattered within an hour.

My patrol of the river had ended without incident and I arrived at the lakes feeling at peace with the world. The sun was now casting long shadows over the water as I entered the top lake; I welcomed the light breeze coming through the pines, scented with the perfume of late summer. A lone angler fished off The Point, an area of bank that juts out like an accusing forefinger, where four young geese paddled aimlessly, looking somewhat confused. Egg-laying dragonflies were gently stabbing the waters with their bodies, in medieval dance. Squirrels busily harvested hazel nuts from the copse with jerky contortions of their fragile frames; whilst overhead continuous flights of birds were weaving in and out of the woods. This was the scene as I made my way upstream.

I was surprised at the lack of anglers, in fact I could make out only three as I rounded a bend in the lake. After spending a little time with the fishermen, all of whom had caught fish, I made my way to the feeder-stream end of the lake: it's a lonely spot where tall reeds, kingcups and giant thistles grace the banks of the narrow stream. Often to be found here is the tall, dignified heron, quietly fishing.

Nearing the stream, cumbersome flapping and an irritable croak told me I had disturbed this bird: but my eyes were drawn to an unfamiliar object alongside the small wooden bridge spanning the stream. There lay the body of an adult Canada goose, the incoming flow buffetting the lifeless form wedged between the rocks. I reached down to remove it from the water. There were no visible signs of damage, only the distended stomach, which suggested possible poisoning; could it have been caused by a freshly sprayed field where the geese grazed?

As I carried the carcase to bury it in the nearby cover of spruce, I noticed the unmistakable enlarged joint of its leg. My goose, Daisy, the one I had rescued three years ago as a gosling. The four young geese downstream were obviously her family. I returned to the roadside after the burial with misty eyes, a three-year friendship ended.

SEPTEMBER 4

Sunshine. Very warm with a slight southerly wind.

River patrol in idyllic conditions. Reports of salmon in the estuary ready to ascend to the spawning grounds. Met today, in a little backwater stretch, the kindly, elderly riparian owner. I was offered a week's salmon fishing which I readily accepted. Saw a lone otter playing in the warm sunshine – must keep quiet about this, their numbers are decreasing each year; mink though are certainly on the increase.

SEPTEMBER 6

Today I had a most heartwarming encounter, the sort of bonus which makes the job even more worthwhile than usual.

A frail lady in her late seventies arrived at the permit office to collect her licence. In a soft cultured voice she enquired about the fishing. She was wearing a tweed suit that hung loosely from her small shoulders; around her neck she wore a thin gold chain anchoring a small naval crown that half disappeared into her delicate, lace-trimmed blouse. A faint fragrance of perfume mingled with the fishy odour of the hut.

With misshapen, rheumatic hands she wrote her permit. After completing the formalities she got into her old Austin Seven, although I wouldn't have been surprised in the least if a carriage and pair had been waiting for her!

Later I began my patrol; there were few anglers, the bulk of holidaymakers having left. The sun was surprisingly warm with just a hint of breeze ruffling the water. Five anglers were fishing the right bank, and the fish were obliging the rods; all was peaceful on a glorious afternoon with the soft sunlight casting long shadows upon the waters.

On the causeway over the Lagoon, I could see the lady fishing alone, casting her fly gently upon the water. She certainly had the touch of an expert. Stopping a few yards away from her I noticed how serene and contented she looked. She appeared to be deep in thought.

I thought it would be wrong for me to disturb her and decided to cut through the woods to reach the other bank which would enable me to continue my patrol. I felt like an intruder as she looked up and gestured for me to join her.

I saw she had caught a small brown trout, which she picked up before making her way to the causeway where there is a large granite boulder. She sat down and started to talk.

She told me that she and her husband, a former R.N. Officer, now dead, had actually become engaged on this very spot. Although after they married she had travelled the world with him, they had always returned to the lakes whenever they could. Suddenly she stopped talking and appeared to be deep in thought. "It's our wedding anniversary today, you know, I do miss him so." She returned her gaze to the water. I felt decidedly embarrassed and finally got up saying, "Duty calls". She appeared not to hear, but just looked at me. Wishing her good fishing I went on my way, eventually reaching the office a little sad.

Several other anglers arrived to fish the evening rise: the waters were covered in masses of shivering rings as the trout began feeding; it looked a promising evening. I leaned over the rail overlooking the lake, casually watching the anglers fishing, when the lady arrived back at the office. I thought she looked tired but happy; she beckoned me over to her car and opened the door. "Howard never forgot our anniversary you see," she said showing me a superb rainbow of five pounds.

SEPTEMBER 10

The mystery of Hamish's teeth is solved. I was walking the banks today when I met a young man coming towards me with a camera slung around his neck. He told me he had captured some superb shots of a vixen and her cubs, and it transpired that he had been up at the back of Bishop's Ripple where the hillside is honeycombed with numerous badger sets; some are many years old, and go back into the hillside for considerable distances.

A vixen and three fox cubs had taken over one of these disused holes, and the photographer had managed to get some good pictures of them at play until they scampered off after being disturbed. At the entrance he had picked up some pale bones. But on closer examination they proved to be a set of false teeth.

When I returned home I telephoned Hamish to tell him of the find but he was unimpressed. "That's all they were fit for, a wee fox," he said. "You might as well give them back to him, he'll have more pleasure out of them than I ever did."

SEPTEMBER 12

The river is running half-spate after the recent rain, and we know the salmon have left the estuary and are heading for the spawning grounds high up on the moor. With the 'run' of fish, poachers are expected to be active, and it was very much with this in mind that today we made our way upstream to a well-known 'holding pool'.

We travelled about three miles to a point where the river takes a sharp bend; large boulders had been placed along the water's edge to compensate for the heavy scouring that frequent floods had caused.

Just a few hundred yards upstream was a superb deep-water pool, where big oaks, with their exposed roots, provide excellent cover for resting migratory fish. We approached the area with stealth. My fellow bailiff touched my arm and said softly, "Smell that – tobacco smoke."

Taking cover behind a mass of brambles we raised our fieldglasses. Nobody was in sight as we scanned the sparkling water upstream; but after a while, not daring to break cover, we saw some orange binder-cord made fast to the roots of an oak. Sure enough, after further study, we could see the tell-tale swirl of water against three beer-bottles acting as floats for the gill net across the pool. We waited and watched.

The sun climbed higher bringing welcome warmth; blue-tits and wagtails flew continuously in and out of the trees, a distant cow was bellowing to her calf, a flash of colour as a kingfisher sped upstream, and all the time the gentle roar of the river as it sped towards the sea. Not a word was spoken between us, only the occasional shifting of our bodies to ease the aches of crouched limbs. Our radios were turned off as we could not afford for our presence to be detected.

The relative calm was disturbed by a mighty splash as what was obviously a fairly large fish became trapped in the net, thrashing the water about fifty yards away. We waited; that's one quality necessary for the job – patience. Fifteen minutes passed, another splash, this time we could make out what looked like a large salmon twisting in the sunlight.

A robin perched on a nearby branch watching expectantly. I was tempted to find an offering from my lunch bag, but I didn't dare open my haversack, every move seemed to be magnified in the tense atmosphere. The bird flew off after a while, apparently disgusted.

A rabbit passed not four yards away, completely unaware of our presence, stopping to savour a choice leaf, nibbling with exaggerated urgency before scampering away.

The tobacco scent once more drifted downstream and we knew our man was not far away, like us he was also watching and waiting. How much longer I thought? My left foot was now dead. I had to ease my leg – the snapping of a twig sounded like a gun-shot! My companion gave me a disapproving look, I shrugged, and pointed to my leg, but he had already returned his gaze upstream. A loud flapping of wings broke the calm, as a startled woodpigeon rose above the trees.

The figure of a man emerged from the deep cover of alder. He was carrying a small orange inflatable and paddle. I was not surprised to see that it was Billy Pyke, whom I'd last encountered in the courtroom at the beginning of the year.

His eyes were intent on the net as he entered the pool and gently paddled across to the opposite bank, not even bothering to look up- or downstream.

We waited and watched him unfasten the net and then drift down, paddling towards the bank where we were hidden, not twenty yards away. I could not deny the excitement I felt as we waited for him to come ashore hauling the net. He was pleased, by the look on his face, as he removed four freshly-run salmon from the net, all from about six to ten pounds in weight.

Quickly he threw the fish into a blue plastic fertilizer bag which he placed in a nearby bush. Expertly he bundled the net and inflatable into a large canvas sack and disappeared into the cover of the woods. We waited for his return while he was hiding his gear.

So silently did he move, literally gliding towards the bush for his catch, that he was upon us before we knew it. Breaking cover we confronted him as he picked up the bag of fish.

"Jesus Christ, not my day today is it?" he said grinning at us. "Hello Billy," I said, "you never learn, do you?" His grin remained fixed but it was devoid of humour. "Arse 'oles!" he retorted, adding insolently, "Got a fag then?"

After charging him we took possession of the fish and asked him for his gear. His reply was unprintable. After a thorough search of the area we found the spot where he had hidden the net. The hiding-place had been used on previous occasions judging by the amount of fish scales adhering to the inside of the old milk churn. It was concealed in a pit some yards from the tree where the net had been made fast. Dead bracken and herbage had been placed across the hole, but the large amount of moisture around the area revealed the hiding-place. We radioed for the Land-Rover to take away the evidence.

The sun sank lower and a decided chill set in as we ate our belated lunch, satisfied.

SEPTEMBER 13

Weather remaining fine.

Tomorrow I begin my salmon fishing week. There should be salmon in the pool waiting for the rains to come. Who knows? I may be lucky.

63

SEPTEMBER 14

A perfect day for fishing. Today I had a remarkable experience with what I have called the 'amorous salmon'.

I arrived beside the river at about ten o'clock. The sun shone through the willows sending dappled reflections on the water, bringing the river alive. Sparkling water meandered gently; all was silent apart from the gurgle of the river thrusting obstinately against the protruding boulders.

Selecting a 'Thunder and Lightning' salmon fly, I gently cast midstream and watched the current slowly carry the brightly coloured bait downstream. Lighting my pipe I was at peace with the world. I continued casting for about an hour with little success; I was not worried, with the utter serenity of the backwater, visits from ever-present birds and an inquisitive heron who, on seeing me, rose laboriously with a rheumatic croak, I was content just to take in the beauty of the September morning.

The faint chimes of the village clock told me it was noon and reeling in my line, I settled down on the bank amid a blaze of campions, their rosy pink contrasting with the lush green of the meadow grass. Pouring myself a coffee I settled back and relaxed, the breeze carrying away little puffs of steam from my cup. I idly watched a magnificent green-and-yellow grass snake silently making its effortless passage through a nearby clump of sedge, the body glistening in the shaded sunlight. Then I noticed a sudden swirl from beside the bole of an ancient oak. It was unmistakable, a freshly-run greenback salmon of about eight pounds, cruising aimlessly. In the clear water I could see that it had a pale scar on its neck about two inches long.

At first I thought it was the first signs of the dreaded U.D.N. disease that has plagued the rivers for the past thirteen years, but after a cautious, closer inspection I confirmed it was a scar of sorts, probably picked up at sea. I gently rose to my feet and cast the fly over its head; it immediately shot away.

After a while I could see the olive green of its body moving towards the bait, it appeared to be playing with it, for it would gently nudge the fly and then disappear upstream and then return for another inspection. I was fascinated by its behaviour, which reminded me of the antics of a sea-lion with a ball. This continued for at least twenty minutes. By then I knew in no way would I be able to entice the salmon to take the fly, nevertheless its playful performance intrigued me. After a while it vanished. I fished on without a take.

I sat down for a lunch-break, this time removing my sea-boots and socks, letting my feet cool in the waters. The sun was high and it was becoming warm. I was halfway through my second sandwich when a most remarkable thing happened. There, literally nudging my toes, was Scar-back. I froze, not daring to move. I felt her – for she was a hen salmon – gently rubbing against my foot. My first reaction was that nobody will ever believe this. I eased my body forward to get a closer look, fully expecting her to shy away, but no, she continued with her caress, for that is what it was.

I reluctantly withdrew my feet, by now they had become cold, and towelled them dry, fully expecting the fish to go, but she still circled close by. I was delighted, in fact so much so, I decided not to fish any more that day. My coffee by now was cold and I replenished my cup, but my appetite had gone. Lighting my pipe I was content to watch this extraordinary fish until she finally returned to the roots of the oak. I was determined to keep this a secret.

SEPTEMBER 15

I arrived at the river an hour earlier than yesterday only to find another angler fishing the precise spot. The disappointment was cruel; however, I exchanged words and he told me that he hadn't had a touch since he arrived over two hours ago. I was wickedly pleased, nevertheless he continued to fish the same spot.

Moving downstream where the river curves, about fifty yards away, I cast my first fly. I could just see the other angler and from time to time I would cast a covetous glance at him, dreading that Scar-back would show herself. I must confess I was behaving strangely.

After about an hour the angler walked towards me saying there was nothing there and that he thought he'd try the weir. I hoped my excitement on my face did not show. Muttering some inane remarks I watched him disappear downstream. My first reaction was to run back to the spot he had left, but I restrained myself for at least ten minutes – which seemed like an hour.

Eagerly casting a 'Thunder and Lightning' I waited for Scar-back. I was so sure somehow she would appear, but alas after thirty minutes not a sign. Telling myself not to be so damned stupid, but feeling downhearted, I reeled in my line and sat down for lunch. The effect on me was staggering, for although the weather was perfect, I could not relax and enjoy the beauty that surrounded me, somehow I had become dissatisfied.

Having finished my lunch, but with no signs of the salmon, I decided to spend just a little while longer before moving downstream. I was about to cast, when right beneath me was Scar-back. Supressing my excitement I slowly placed the rod on the bank and quietly knelt down to put my hand into the water. She immediately moved out to midstream. Calling softly, as one would call one's favourite cat, I gently rippled the water with my fingers. Scar-back hesitated, turned, and cautiously moved slowly towards my hand.

Still calling softly, the salmon passed gently under my hand, and I began to caress her back. She hardly moved, except for a slight flexing of the tail to keep her head to the current.

We remained like that for about three minutes. My back began to ache but I dared not move. Then for no reason she flicked her tail vigorously and shot back under the oak. I was thrilled, staying for at least another hour, but she refused to show herself. My desire for further fishing that day was gone. I left for home elated.

SEPTEMBER 20

Overcast threatening rain.

I have seen Scar-back twice more during the week, going through the same ritual of calling her and stroking her back. I haven't told a soul, for it is indeed an experience to be cherished.

SEPTEMBER 24

The rains have arrived.

Heavy torrential rain has sent the river in full spate. Scar-back must be well on her way upstream to the spawning grounds. I hope she survives.

SEPTEMBER 30

The season is drawing to a close and the whole countryside is beginning to change, with lush green giving way to a mellow, ruddy bronze. Already the telegraph wires are lined with chattering swallows, mustering into convoys for their flight to the sun. The trees stand silent in the still air, heavy branches full of yellowing leaves, about to begin their winter rest.

Smoke hangs heavy over the valley from burning stubble, and the evening air echoes to the sound of busy tractors heavily laden with the harvest. Man seems to be the only animal engaged in any activity as the fields, shorn and brown, await the plough before the snow.

The rivers are low and barely moving as they await the autumn rains which will allow the salmon and peal to begin their tortuous journeys to their birthplace amidst the barren moorland wastes. The whole cycle begins once more; fish will spawn, poachers plan their secret and lucrative journeys to the spawning grounds, and bailiffs prepare for nightly encounters. Nothing really alters.

Today I am receiving a consignment of next year's fish. Thousands of diminutive fingerlings which will need constant attention during the coming months. They need to be fed regularly, cossetted and protected from the herons. I have seen one enterprising heron kneel down and thrust his beak into a small opening of the protective net in order to reach the succulent, unsuspecting trout, only to be thwarted after spending several minutes in the uncomfortable, unnatural stance.

Cormorants will soon be travelling inland to establish territorial fishing areas, but although the amount of prime fish these predators consume is considerable, and obviously they are not welcomed by private commercial fisheries, I must say that, to me, they add a certain charm to the lakes on an autumn morning. Diving amongst the rocks and squatting in rows with outstretched wings drying in the wind they look like a row of gothic gargoyles. But they are certainly costly to the Authority.

September is a good month to observe the ever-changing sky over the moor. From my hillside home I have an uninterrupted view of some miles, where green patterned fields merge with heather-clad hills, and the river meanders through the valley. Often huge black clouds spill over the skyline, and while solid sheets of rain sweep across half the area, the remainder basks in soft sunlight. But then that's Dartmoor weather.

OCTOBER 3

Fine, sunny, southerly wind.

At last I can see some sunshine. The rainbow fishing has been extended until the end of the month at the lakes. Today I met an angler who was certainly worth noting.

He arrived at the permit office in style. The long, silver Daimler purred to a stop, and from its polished body emerged a man of medium height, portly and dressed in a good tweed fishing suit, complete with long woollen stockings and green tab garters. These set off a pair of expensive brown-leather shoes, as tough as elephant's hide.

The visitor's silver hair was slightly ruffled on a head that appeared to have no neck. I said good morning but he ignored the courtesy and in the tone of a squire addressing one of his workers told me he wanted to fish the lake. I began to explain the procedure and offered a word of advice, as I do to all those I take to be newcomers to the waters. But his only reply was an occasional grunt of an irritable "Yes! Yes!" He never looked at me for more than a brief second during the whole meeting.

He wrote out his permit and without a second glance at me he strode out, got back into his car, and drove off at speed for the car-park. A friendly chap if ever I saw one!

During the afternoon patrol of the lake I came upon him fishing the Bay; he was taking a swig from a flask. I asked if he had any success?

"No I haven't!" he exploded. "I don't believe there's any bloody fish in the lake!" I discreetly walked on, finishing my patrol an hour later.

Anglers were returning to the office with their fish to have them recorded. Two fish was about the average as the temperature was falling sharply and the fish had gone deep; no longer a productive period of the day.

At five o'clock a young lad of about thirteen arrived to weigh his catch: five prime rainbows with one weighing six pounds plus. He was a good angler having caught at least two hundred fish during the season; he was pleased with himself. I was measuring the large trout when the Daimler driver walked in the door. His face was a study. Looking, or rather glaring, first at the large rainbow and then at the remaining four, he turned to the lad and exclaimed with apparent disbelief, "Did you – emphasis on the 'you' – catch those?"

"Yes, sir," the boy answered respectfully.

"What did you catch them on? eh? Maggots?" said the man.

"No, sir, all on black lures." I could see that the young lad was becoming distressed. I put the fish in the boy's bag and gently ushered him to the door. But the man was not finished with me yet, although as he looked me straight in the eyes for the first time, I noticed that all the venom had left his face. "I've fished all over Scotland, Ireland, and even America you know. But I come here for the first time and it's taken a mere slip of a boy to show me how to fish."

Before I could explain to him that I've seen it happen time and time again he went on, "This is the final bloody straw! My wife's left me, my children refuse to speak to me, and on the way here I got a bloody puncture."

There was not really much I could say. He turned and left the office and I heard him drive off. A little later an angler came in carrying an expensive cane rod, broken in four jagged pieces. He told me he had found it down the road and thought it had probably been run over.

NOVEMBER 1

Soon the first frosts will arrive and trigger off the spawning season.

I look forward to the long treks along the rivers, even though at times they can be hazardous. The exhilaration of the high moorland air and the intense peacefulness of Dartmoor bring an inner comfort to the entire senses.

NOVEMBER 6

Tomorrow we are going to the hatchery to strip some rainbows. I really am looking forward to this.

NOVEMBER 7

Tom was waiting at the massive iron gates to the hatchery when the twelve bailiffs from different parts of the county arrived. He was pleased to see us, for looking after a hatchery can be lonely at times and Tom is a man who likes a good jaw.

He directed us to two large circular bowls situated away from the main tanks. These contained large, brood rainbow trout, hens in one and cocks in the other, swimming around like submarines.

One young bailiff appeared to be a little apprehensive when told to enter the tank with two of his colleagues, asking "Do they bite?" He tried to make it sound like a joke but he seemed a bit hesitant, perched with one leg over the edge of the concrete bowl. Jan got hold of his shoulder saying, "You won't feel much, not through yer waders," and pulled him in.

With a swirl of frothy water, the fish immediately swam to the far end of the tank. The routine was to catch a hen weighing somewhere in the region of ten pounds plus, and gently but firmly tuck its head under your arm, thus shielding its eyes. This quietens the fish so you can grasp the tail and at the same time slightly arch the fish's back. With the forefinger and thumb you then firmly rub along the underside of the trout to the vent.

The small orange eggs exude from the vent and are directed into a dry bowl. You then select a cock fish from the other tank – easier said than done – and repeat the exercise letting the milt cover the eggs in the bowl. It is best to use two cock fish to ensure fertilization of the eggs.

After replacing the fish gently back into the water, the eggs and milt are gently stirred and clean water is added to half-fill the bowl. The bowl is covered for a quarter of an hour and then the surplus milt and egg shells are washed off from the hardened eggs. The eggs are then incubated.

By lunchtime we had finished our stripping. In twelve months' time, if all goes well, those eggs will be rainbow trout of a pound each, ready for stocking the lakes.

NOVEMBER 15

Tomorrow David and I will make our first survey; already snow clouds are sweeping in off the moor. The forecast says possible light snow showers – I hope they will be light.

NOVEMBER 16

The weather forecast was right for a change. The high tors on the moor are covered with a light sprinkling of snow, as if a giant shaker of icing-sugar had been sifted over the countryside. Winter has come.

Spawning time: already the salmon and sea-trout are beginning to arrive at the upper reaches of the seven rivers that rise on the moor.

Heron and cormorants are leaving the estuaries to take easy pickings from the inland lakes. Overhead, buzzards make their continuous search, wheeling high in the morning sky, uttering their kitten-like mewing cries.

Today David and I began our seasonal pilgrimage, searching for redds in the narrow fast-moving streams of this fairyland of rugged beauty. A keen north-west wind swept over the moor while the pale watery sun tried its hardest to warm us as we stumbled over the granite boulders that clutter the narrow waters. A kingfisher was playing hide and seek with its mate as we came to our first salmon redd.

Salar the salmon, wearing her dark-red livery, was already at work weaving and turning in her endeavour to make a bed for her unborn amidst the small round pebbles. Nearby an anxious cock, complete with its fearsome kype*, waited to fertilize the future generation. We knew we were witnessing a scene that had been taking place since time began.

---

* *Kype – the hooked lower jaw developed on a male salmon at spawning time.*

70

David pointed to the hen, which had already made a fair-sized hole. Across the other side of the stream two young rabbits watched us like inquisitive children wrapped in their winter coats. The hen appeared satisfied with her labours and released a mass of tiny orange eggs over the hole. I watched fascinated as the bright pearls settled gently in the redd. The cold clear water was disturbed as the cock quickly swam across the eggs, releasing its milky fluid and clouding the water. The life process had begun.

The hen swam upstream where she began weaving and turning, disturbing the gravel which the strong flow soon carried into the depression, leaving a mound of stones over the redd.

An hour later we reached the end of our search and crossed the moor to follow another stream down to the confluence of the river. Here we were in luck. David pointed to a pair of otters playing amongst the rocks; in the middle of the river was a large boulder occupied by a dipper bird. "Sip, sip," it called. We stopped to watch it. Already a mist was creeping in, its cold penetrating the very bones.

Hastening our steps, we made our way down the valley past an ancient hut circle. Soon we could smell the warm comforting woodsmoke drifting over the evening air. Home was not far away. It was dusk when we finally arrived, tired but satisfied, to piping-hot pie before a log fire.

I will sleep tonight with only the hooting of an owl disturbing the deathly hush of a Dartmoor night.

NOVEMBER 17

An amazing experience today as David and I continue our search for redds up on the moors. Almost unbelievable. But David was there and saw it too.

We left for the moor in the cold chill of the morning and finally plodded our way to the first stop, a narrow sweep of river with a gravelled bed where the water was shallow, clear and fast-moving – ideal for spawning. There was no immediate sign of any redds but as we scanned the water for any movements of fish, David touched my arm without speaking and pointed to a swirl. There, unmistakably were two ferocious-looking cock salmon, their ugly kypes thrusting upwards, slowly keeping station against the flow. But then the hen came into view. I froze. It was Scar-back!

I just didn't believe it at first but there was no mistaking the distinctive mark on the neck that had led me to name her so. We watched as she made her redd. It took at least an hour before she finally deposited her eggs in the shallow depression. I still wasn't quite able to take in the fact that, of all the salmon in all the miles of river here on the moor, we should meet again.

After the eggs had been fertilized, Scar-back swam upstream to move the pebbles over her eggs. We later followed to where she was resting and with my heart in my mouth I knelt down at the water's edge and began to call softly, at the same time moving my hand in the bitterly cold river. Scar-back did not move. I felt disappointed. David looked at me strangely. "You've got some hope; you can tickle a trout but not a salmon," he said. I wanted to tell him my experience of the previous month but somehow I couldn't.

I remained for about fifteen minutes, withdrawing my hand every so often as it became numb. David was getting impatient with me, for it was getting cold. And then, as if she had caught my scent Scar-back cruised under my hand and allowed me a quick caress.

"Bugger me!" exclaimed David. As we continued on our way upstream, I told him of the past encounter with Scar-back and for the rest of the day all I could get out of him was "Bugger me!"

NOVEMBER 23

Frost, severe. Light airs.

Spawning patrols continue; by the number of redds that have been recorded it looks good, but I can't help wondering, although there should be a good harvest of fry, how many will reach maturity. How many will survive not only the natural predators, but the unnatural – man-predators?

Reports from all rivers are excellent.

DECEMBER 4

The countryside is still in the grip of the bitterly cold weather.

Rivers are now running at reduced flow and there is evidence that many salmon and sea-trout have been over-cutting. This means fish are making redds, one on top of another. In a way I suppose its not all that bad, for when the river spates many redds will be flattened but at least some will survive.

DECEMBER 12

The rains have arrived. Winds south-west, force 7.

At last the rivers are in spate and the frost has vanished.

Patrols are now confined to anti-poaching. The skeletal branches of the trees stand bare: the last remaining leaves are scattered. Birds huddle in the crevices of trees, seeking what shelter they can get from the lashing wind. The countryside has begun its winter sleep. Cattle gather in forlorn company along the hedgerows, their rain-soaked coats steaming in the morning air.

We bailiffs plod the river bank where a family of duck gather in a backwater, completely indifferent to the deluge, dipping and jostling.

Soon I know the trees will bud and birds will begin building their nests: spring will come, transforming the whole country into a wonderland of unequalled beauty. Once more we shall see the deep Devon lanes smothered in celandines, scabious, lady's smock, campion and stately foxgloves; the woodlands carpeted with a million bluebells.

River banks will be clad with fragile ferns and mosses while the first flush of daffodils and primroses transforms the streams and waterways. Yes, I have a lot to look forward to in the new year.

Tomorrow I begin my outstanding leave.

Oh, the wisher winter evenings, when the dimsy comes down grey an' the air be offering the snow, an' the mind be full of old sad tales of the dead an' gone.

4
ENVOI
SCAR-BACK'S RETURN

THE rain has come at last, bringing welcomed relief to the countryside; but most important of all to the rivers.

Long parched days have upset the migratory run of the Salmonids, resulting in shoals of salmon and sea-trout waiting in the estuaries to begin their journeys to the spawning-grounds. Poachers are having a field day, especially with the high prices that salmon fetch today.

I had walked the rivers only to find cobbled beds barely covered with water; just enough to give life to the stonefly and boatman spiders.

With the rain, a fast, full flow now washes away the summer debris of dead foliage, empty cans and other refuse. Once again the pools are filled with the swirling forms of fish on their way up to the spawning grounds. What a grand sight they make as they swim up river. This pilgrimage has taken place since time began, and still man is baffled as to how they manage to navigate to their birthplace, in spite of many theories that have been put forward.

I am going to follow Scar-back in an imaginary journey to the moor, describing the hazards that she will encounter.

It was on the spawning grounds two winters ago that I last saw her, laying her eggs amongst the gravel beds. She has since returned to the sea, arriving once more at the mouth of the Teign in October after a two year spell feeding in the rich krill waters off the Icelandic coast. After waiting in the estuary for her body to undergo the osmotic changes that are necessary for her body to adapt from salt to fresh-water, she was ready to begin her journey.

Scar-back had managed to avoid the many nets strung across the entrance to the river. Now the full force of the spate drew her over the treacherous sandbar, past the bobbing boats and under the wide bridge spanning the river. As the estuary narrowed she knew that the real dangers lay ahead.

The sky darkened, with the moon shining fitfully through the scudding clouds as she made for the first pool where she knew she could rest. She moved at speed.

Sometime later Scar-back arrived at weir-pool bridge where an ancient oak spread its branches across the deep water. She settled herself beneath the roots, with just an occasional flick of her tail to keep her head-on to the flow. She was tired. The sky had cleared and the moon cast shadows of the willows upon the still water of the pool.

Scar-back was alerted by the urgent, furtive movement of three men as they set a net across the pool. She lay still as the shadowy pattern of the net slowly sank to the bed of the river. All was quiet, only the distant rush of water over the weir disturbed the silence of the night. She forced herself more tightly into the roots and waited.

An hour had passed; Scar-back eased herself forward into midstream, her dorsal fin had become wedged in a downward bend of a root and she wanted more oxygen. She turned and faced the flow moving her tail just enough to keep her in station. There she dozed.

Two salmon and a large sea-trout swimming strongly up river, failed to see the net and crashed headlong into the mesh. The frantic vibrations of their struggle to escape reached Scar-back who retreated quickly back into shelter.

The turmoil at the net continued for minutes and Scar-back pressed still further into the dark, sinewy roots: she instinctively knew that danger threatened, but how much longer could she hold out? The lack of oxygen was beginning to tell and in desperation she gave a gigantic thrust of her body and shot out once more into midstream, swimming back downstream to stop just a little way from the fall of the weir.

All was now quiet at the net, only an occasional last desperate slap from the exhausted and dying fish. Scar-back could see stars and a bright moon shining through the branches. There were no signs of the men, only the gaunt outline of a heron fishing the tail of the weir for parr. She felt easier now with the full body of water flowing past her gills: she rested and waited, tired, so tired. An hour later she cautiously returned to the oak and settled herself for the rest of the night.

The thin, shrill piping of a robin awoke her from her reverie: at dawn the poachers returned to the river and Scar-back watched their shadowy forms removing the net, their gruff voices commenting on their illegal catch.

All day, Scar-back continued her voyage along the ribbons of water, eventually reaching a stickle about half a mile from the pass. There she sought refuge underneath an outcrop of granite jutting out in the river some twenty yards from New Bridge. Here the water swirled and washed the ancient, mossy flagstones of the small, humped-back bridge.

That night it became cold as the crescent moon bathed the water in a soft light, mellow and comforting. Three sea-trout decided to keep Scar-back company during the silent hours, disturbed only by the hooting of an old tawny owl that stood sentry in a nearby sycamore.

With the coming of the dawn, Scar-back saw that the sea-trout had gone, with a twist of her tail she entered mid-river and headed for the weir. Here the river meandered through meadows where bullocks grazed, their breath puffing little pockets of vapour into the sunlit air.

The drop in temperature urged Scar-back on: Her belly, full of thousands of orange pearls, hung heavily beneath her twelve-pound body. Instinct urged her on and on. Although the river was now beginning to drop, it was vital for her to jump the weir for her next resting pool.

Other young salmon now joined her, their plump bodies glistening in the pale sunshine with sea-lice still nestling around the gills, for these had arrived within two days from the sea. Each fish was now intent on ascending the pass before the levels dropped any further.

One lone angler could be seen casting his bait expectantly towards the narrow fish-pass tucked away on the far side of the weir. Scar-back waited, cruising to and fro at the base of the rock-strewn dam bubbling with white water. She became intoxicated with the heavily-charged oxygen.

The fisherman increased his casting, dropping the artificial minnow over her nose where it flashed as it was being spun through the water. She refused to be tempted, although she was becoming irritated, for the salmon by nature is a natural predator. But in a flash one of the young salmon took the Devon-minnow in its jaws, momentarily jerking to a halt. It was well and truly hooked as it took the line downstream, its body weaving and turning in a futile attempt to dislodge the barbed imitation fish. Scar-back mustered all her strength and, on the third attempt, cleared the weir landing with a loud splash in the slow-moving waters of the pool.

The sun tried its hardest to break through the high mist, for the banks of the river were now steaming as the dew rose in the morning air. The constant roar of the motorway traffic seemed unreal, sending shattering waves of noise through the water. Scar-back knew she must seek the safer and quieter part of the river. There she rested uneasily amongst the reeds, whose roots housed the eggs of the damsel flies that would grace next summer's waters. Scar-back was living off her body fat and would not eat until she returned to the sea. Her last meal, some weeks ago, had been of herring caught in the channel. She cautiously left the cover of the reeds and headed upstream, leaving behind two fishermen who were now fishing the run downstream of the weir, encouraged by their earlier catch. The sun had disappeared over the moor and the river was now running at a reduced flow; smudges of black midge danced over the water as Scar-back made for the huge concrete bridge that led to the motorway.

She swam close to the bank where straggly clumps of reed offered cover, soon arriving at the bend of the river under the bridge. Some schoolboys were crouching low over the water on the other side of the white mass of concrete. Scar-back swam head first into a loop of wire hanging just beneath the bank. A sudden jerk confused and panicked her as she felt herself being pulled up from the water. Amidst the excited voices of the boys she was clumsily dragged on to a rock.

Half-stunned, and tortured by the lack of oxygen, she gave an almighty twist and slid from the hand grasping her tail. Back into the water she crashed with the snare still around her, swimming swiftly for the middle of the river.

The salmon swam on until evening, trailing the cumbersome snare behind her. Alongside the river, chimney stacks were silhouetted against the darkening sky; here the water exposed small islands of pebbles as the river divided into tiny rivulets.

Scar-back found a rusty iron stake deeply embedded into the silty river bottom and began to rub her flanks against it, sending rusty particles tumbling into the water like ash from a cigar. The choking effect of the wire eased a little but it remained in place. For several hours she worked at her painful, tiring labours; she was becoming exhausted. Abruptly she left the stanchion and made for the sanctuary of a discarded boiler that lay on the bottom of the river. There she rested uneasily.

A tremendous crash, followed by a heavy downpour of rain shook her into life as a storm burst overhead. The whole river became alive as torrential rain boiled upon the surface of the water. Frequent flashes of lightning cast grotesque shadows upon the water as Scar-back looked upwards. She moved quickly to the stickle of gravel where, once again, she began scraping her body against the stones to rid herself of the snare. Overhead the storm intensified.

Her continued working disturbed large pebbles which fell away into the increasing flow. The wire had become much looser now and was very near her tail, but her body was torn where the continued rubbing had chaffed her mangled scales. Then, a final twist released the snare and Scar-back experienced the same feeling she had when ridding herself of parasitic lampreys that so often plague salmon.

Scar-back continued upstream. The flow had now become strong, carrying broken driftwood and silt which discoloured the turbulent water. She instinctively knew that she was safe for the time being. Two sea-trout and a salmon joined her and the little convoy journeyed up the eddying river accompanied by loud claps of thunder.

During the next weeks, Scar-back completed almost two-thirds of her quest, alternately resting between long and arduous stretches, especially when at times she was unable to make progress due to shallows.

By now the river was running half-bank height, being kept at a steady flow by frequent downpours. Scar-back arrived at County Bridge where the river narrows like an hourglass, rushing through the arches of the grey seventeenth-century bridge while modern coaches roar overhead.

Further upstream, the salmon leapt the weir that brought her into clear water running through a deep moorland gorge, home of fallow deer, badger and fox. Here stone-age dwellers had lived and hunted: on such a morning one could envisage fur-clad men fishing the banks to supplement their meagre diets.

A rosette of cotton-wool fungus now grew over the damaged scales of Scar-back; cold temperatures having encouraged the growth. She swam up the valley following the course of many other fish fixed with the same urgency to spawn. This was otter country; Scar-back must now be on the alert.

By evening she had arrived at Moor Bridge. It had become very dark and bitterly cold, but no moon shone over this notorious length of river, which poachers had christened their 'piggy-bank'. Here water-bailiffs patrolled in strength in the never-ending fight against the greed and violence of organized gangs.

Scar-back decided to spend the night in the shelter of some oaks whose great exposed roots burrowed deep in the pool. There she settled, the water spilling over the weir lulling her senses.

Dawn's first pale gleam lightened the eastern sky and Scar-back, finding difficulty in breathing, became distressed. She knew something was wrong and that she must leave immediately.

The water had become devoid of life-giving oxygen. Surfacing, Scar-back saw several fish drifting downstream on their backs, mouths wide open, gasping in the throes of death. The river was being poached with chemicals.

Scar-back quickly dropped back over the weir downstream, seeking fresher water. She could hear a commotion on the banks upstream, where men with long gaffs were stabbing the waters, their excited voices shattered the stillness of the morning. Scar-back retreated still further taking refuge under the bridge where the crackling of a bailiff's radio directed and received messages.

Looking up Scar-back saw a dark shape moving in the water towards her. For a second she mistook the movement for an otter, but it was too cumbersome.

Then a gruff voice shouted, "It's all right down here, thank Christ. I can see one swimming about, thank God it's clear this far!" It was the voice of a bailiff.

Later that morning, the river now clear of the last trace of chemicals, Scar-back continued her journey, once again entering the pool and swimming on towards the moor. Now she left behind the poisoned water from which the poachers had so wickedly attempted to harvest their illegal catch; only to be thwarted by the diligence of the water-bailiffs.

Nearing Fingle Bridge, Scar-back passed several salmon with fungus-covered bodies; some were lying between the sides of fallen trees being buffeted by eddies in a little back-water. She caught the merest glimpse of an otter slipping into the water and disappearing from sight.

Scar-back swam past the cattle crossing where frost-filled hoof prints patterned the sloping bank. Just one more weir to cross and her journey would end. Already the cock fish were loitering on the gravel beds awaiting the arrival of the mother fish.

Scar-back went straight over the pass with little difficulty and made for a shallow feeder stream. Already several little mounds could be seen where other salmon had spawned. Scar-back set to work with little delay excavating a suitable site; her body and tail weaving and turning, sending the pebbles downstream; the reddish gold of her flanks glinting in the pale sunlight.

Between rests she was finally satisfied with her labours and swam over the depression releasing hundreds of tiny orange eggs which tumbled gently down. An attendant cock salmon, looking ferocious with its fully-grown kype, immediately swam over the redd releasing spurts of thin milky fluid that caressed the eggs.

Scar-back swam a little way upstream and, using her tail, created a turbulence sending pebbles downstream to fall into the depression, forming a small mound.

She re-enacted the same ritual twice more during the next two days before completing her spawning. Now she was thoroughly exhausted, her body lean and hungry. She had now reached the 'kelt' stage, recognized as an unclean fish under the Salmon and Freshwater Fisheries Act.

The following weeks saw heavy rain, bringing the already swollen rivers into full spate. Scar-back drifted lazily with the flow of muddy water, easing her passage down towards the estuary. Gradually her strength returned, her body growing deep and silver as she swam rapidly towards the sea.

Called by the crash of breakers, Scar-back entered the Channel in late December heading out towards the Atlantic. Behind her, black against the night sky, rose the cliffs of Devon where the Berry Head Light blinked farewell against the starry sky.